JOSEPH

Loved, Despised and Exhalted

AMBASSADOR

BELFAST, NORTHERN IRELAND
GREENVILLE, USA

JOSEPH
Loved, Despised and Exhalted

F. B. Meyer

AMBASSADOR

BELFAST, NORTHERN IRELAND
GREENVILLE, USA

Joseph - Loved, Despised and Exhalted
This edition 2003

ISBN 1   84030 137 6

Ambassador Publications
a division of
Ambassador Productions Ltd.
Providence House
Ardenlee Street,
Belfast,
BT6 8QJ
Northern Ireland
www.ambassador-productions.com

Emerald House
427 Wade Hampton Blvd.
Greenville
SC 29609, USA
www.emeraldhouse.com

PREFACE

MY first essay at Scripture Biography was made on the Life of Joseph. And ever since Joseph's life has had a special charm for me, not only for its intrinsic beauty, but because of its vivid anticipations of the Life that lights all lives.

I remember seeing the huge Matterhorn reflected, in its minutest details, in a small mountain lakelet, many miles distant; and similarly, the life of Jesus is remarkably mirrored in this touching story.

In fact, there are scenes in the life of Joseph which probably foreshadow events that are timed to happen in the near future, and which depict them with a vividness and minuteness not to be found elsewhere on the page of Scripture. It is here only that we can fully realize what will take place when the Lord Jesus makes Himself known to his brethren according to the flesh, and they exclaim, "It is Jesus our brother!"

F. B. MEYER.

CONTENTS

I

EARLY DAYS

(GENESIS XXXVII)

"Behind our life the Weaver stands
And works his wondrous will;
We leave it all in his wise hands,
And trust his perfect skill.
Should mystery enshroud his plan,
And our short sight be dim,
We will not try the whole to scan,
But leave each thread to Him."
C. MURRAY.

IT was said by Coleridge that our greatest mission is to rescue admitted truths from the neglect caused by their universal admission. There is much force in this. When a truth is fighting for existence, it compels men, whether they love it or not, to consider it. But when its position is secured, it becomes like a well-used coin, or the familiar text which hangs unnoticed on the wall. It is a great mission to rescue such truths from neglect; to flash upon them the strong light which arrests attention; to play the part of Old Mortality, who, chisel in hand, was wont to clear the mould of neglect from the gravestones of the Covenanters, so that the legend might stand out clear-cut. It is something like this that I attempt for this exquisite story. We think we know all about it; and yet there may be depths of meaning and beauty which, by their very familiarity, escape us. Let us ponder together the story of JOSEPH; and as we do so, we shall get many a foreshadowing of Him who was cast into the pit of death, and who now sits at the right hand of Power, a Prince and a Saviour.

I. THE FORMATIVE INFLUENCES OF HIS EARLY LIFE.—Seventeen years before our story opens, a little child was borne by Rachel, the favourite wife of Jacob. The latter was then living as manager for his uncle Laban, on the ancient pasture-land of Charran, situated in the valley of the Euphrates and the Tigris, from which his grandfather Abraham had been called by God. The child received an eager welcome from its parents, and from the first gave unusual promise. He was like one of those children, whom we sometimes meet in large families, who bear a marked contrast to the rest; and who grow up like some fair Saxon child amid the swarthy natives of a tent of gipsies who have made it their prize.

But what a history has passed in that interval! When yet a child he was hastily caught up by his mother, and sustained in her arms on the back of a swift camel, urged to its highest speed, in the flight across the desert that lay, with only one oasis, between the bank of the Euphrates and the green prairies of Gilead. He could just remember the panic that spread through the camp when tidings came that Esau, the dread uncle, was on his march, with four hundred followers. Nor could he ever forget the evening full of preparation, the night of solemn expectancy, and the morning when his father limped into the camp, maimed in body, but with the look of a prince upon his face.

More recently still, he could recall the hurried flight from the enraged idolaters of Shechem; and those solemn hours at Bethel where his father had probably showed him the very spot on which the foot of the mystic ladder had rested, and where the whole family formally entered into a new covenant with God. It may be that this was the turning point of his life. Such events make deep impressions on young hearts. As they stood together on that hallowed spot, and heard again the oft-told story, and clasped each other's hands in solemn covenant, the other sons of Jacob may have been unmoved spectators; but there was a deep response in the susceptible heart of the lad, who may have felt, "This God shall be my

God for ever and ever; He shall be my Guide, even unto death."

If this were so, these impressions were soon deepened by three deaths. When they reached the family settlement, they found the old nurse Deborah dying. She was the last link to those bright days when her young mistress Rebekah came across the desert to be Isaac's bride; and they buried her with many tears under an ancient but splendid oak. And he could never forget the next. The long caravan was moving slowly up to the narrow ridge along which lay the ancient village of Bethlehem: suddenly a halt was called; the beloved Rachel could go not another step; there as the sun was westering, amid scenes where in after-years Ruth met Boaz, and David watched his sheep, and the good Joseph walked beside the patient ass with its precious burden—there Rachel, Joseph's mother, died. This was the greatest loss that he had ever known. A little while after, the lad stood with his father and brethren before Machpelah's venerable grave, to lay Isaac where Abraham and Sarah and Rebekah awaited him, each on a narrow shelf; and where, after a space of seven-and-twenty years, he was to place the remains of his father Jacob.

These things made Joseph what he was. And the little sympathy that he received from his family only drove him more apart, and compelled him to live "by the well" (Gen. xlix. 22), and to strike his roots deeper into the life of God.

It may be that these words will be read by youths of seventeen who have passed through experiences not unlike Joseph's. They have lost sainted friends. They have been emptied from vessel to vessel. They feel lonely in the midst of their home. Let me solemnly ask them if they have entered into covenant with God. Have you avouched God to be your God? Have you put your hand into the hand of "the mighty God of Jacob"? It is an urgent question, for the answer to it may mark the crisis of your lives. Choose Christ; and, in choosing Him, choose life, and blessedness, and heaven. And when you have chosen Him, cleave close to Him, and send the rootlets of your existence deep down into the hidden wells of communion and fellowship.

II. THE EXPERIENCES OF HIS HOME LIFE.—*Joseph was endowed with very remarkable intelligence.* It would almost seem as if he were chief shepherd (ver. 2), the sons of Bilhah and Zilpah acting as his subordinates and assistants. The Rabbis describe him as a wise son, endowed with knowledge beyond his years. It was this, combined with the sweetness of his disposition, and the memory of his mother, that won for him his father's peculiar love. "Israel loved Joseph more than all his children."

And this love provided the coat of many colours. We have been accustomed to think of this coat as a kind of patchwork quilt, and we have wondered that grown men should have been moved to so much passion at the sight of the peacock plumes of their younger brother. But further knowledge will correct these thoughts. The Hebrew word means simply a tunic reaching to the extremities, and describes a garment commonly worn in Egypt and the adjacent lands. Imagine a long white linen robe extending to the ankles and wrists, and embroidered with a narrow stripe of colour round the edge of the skirt and sleeves, and you will have a very fair conception of this famous coat.

Now we can understand the envy of his brothers. This sort of robe was worn only by the opulent and noble, by kings' sons, and by those who had no need to toil for their living. All who had to win their bread by labour wore short, coloured garments that did not show stain, or cramp the free movement of the limbs. Such was the lot of Jacob's sons, and such the garments they wore. They had to wade through morasses, to clamber up hills, to carry wandering sheep home on their shoulders, to fight with robbers and beasts of prey; and for such toils the flowing robe would have been quite unfit. But when Jacob gave such a robe to Joseph, he declared in effect that from such hardships and toils his favourite son should be exempt. Now in those times the father's will was law. When, therefore, they saw Joseph tricked out in his robe of state, the brethren felt that in all likelihood *he* would have the rich inheritance, whilst *they* must follow a life of toil. "And when his brethren saw that their father loved him more than all his brethren, they hated him, and could not speak peaceably unto him."

The case was aggravated by his plain speaking. "He brought unto his father their evil report." At first sight this does not seem a noble trait in his character. Love covereth the multitude of sins, as the two elder sons of Noah covered their father's shame. At the same time there may have been circumstances that justified, and even demanded, the exposure. It is sometimes the truest kindness, after due and repeated warning, to expose the evil deeds of those with whom we live and work. If they are permitted to go on in sin, apparently undetected, they will become hardened and emboldened, and eager to go to greater lengths. Moreover, Joseph was probably placed over them, and was responsible to his father for their behaviour. He was jealous for the family name, which they had already "made to stink among the inhabitants of the land." He was eager for the glory of God, whose name was continually blasphemed through their means. And, therefore, without attempting to conceal the evil, he told their father just how matters stood.

But this was enough to make them hate him. "Every one that doeth evil hateth the light." "I hate him," said the infuriated Ahab when speaking of Micaiah, "because he doth not prophesy good of me, but evil." "The world cannot hate you," our Lord said sadly; "but Me it hateth, because I testify of it, that its works are evil." So will it be always: if the world loves us and speaks well of us, we may gravely question if we are salt, pure and stinging, amid its corruption, or lights in its midnight gloom. As soon as our lives become a strong contrast and reproof, we shall arouse its undying hate. "What evil have I done," said the ancient Cynic, "to make all men speak well of me?"

But still further, *Joseph dreamed that he should become the centre of the family life.* All young people dream. Unless our lot has been peculiarly hard and untoward, we all, in the sunny days of youth, don Joseph's tunic, and dream—how great and successful we shall be!—how noble and heroic!—how much good we are to get and give! The heavens shall rain soft showers of benediction! The earth shall yield flowers for our feet and fruits to our taste! We shall surpass all who have preceded us; sitting on the throne of supremacy, whilst our detractors and foes do us obeisance! Alas, our raiment soon drips with blood, and we find ourselves down in the pit, or sold into captivity. But there was this in Joseph's dreams, they foretold not only his exaltation, but his brothers' humiliation. If he were the central sheaf, their sheaves must do obeisance, by falling to the earth around it. If he were on the throne, sun, moon, and stars must do him homage. This was more than the proud spirits of his brethren could brook, and "they hated him yet the more."

But the root of their enmity lay even deeper. In Eden, when addressing the serpent, God said: "I will put enmity between thee and the woman, and between thy seed and her seed." That is one of the profoundest sayings in the Bible. It is the key to Scripture. All that comes after only proves the virulence and the universality of the conflict between the children of God and the children of the devil. It broke out between Cain and Abel. It has embittered every family. It has rent every home. It shall yet convulse the universe. This was the secret of the conflict that raged around Joseph. I grant that the home was ill-organized; that all the evils incident to polygamy were there; that Jacob was incompetent to rule. But still I see there an instance of that conflict of which Christ spake: "I am come to set a man at variance against his father, and the daughter against her mother; . . . and a man's foes shall be they of his own household."

Do you know by sad experience what Joseph felt beneath those Syrian skies? Do the archers shoot at you? Are you lonesome and depressed, and ready to give up? Take heart! —see the trampled grass and the snapped twigs; others have gone this way before you. Christ your Lord suffered the same treatment from His own. Go on doing right, in nothing terrified by your adversaries. Be pitiful and gentle, forgiving and forbearing. Be specially careful not to take your case into your own hands; demanding redress in imperious and vindictive tones. If you are servants, forbear to answer back. Give your backs to the smiters, and your cheeks to them that pluck off the hair. Avenge not yourselves, but rather give place unto wrath. Put down your feet into the footprints of your Saviour, who left an example that we should follow Him. He did no sin, neither was guile found in His mouth: and yet, when He was unjustly reviled, He reviled not again; when He suffered beneath undeserved contumely and reproach, He did not even remind the perpetrators of the righteous judgment of God, but was dumb as a lamb, and threatened not, and committed Himself to Him that judgeth righteously.

And what was the result? Joseph was carried through the hatred and opposition of his foes; and his dreams were literally fulfilled in the golden days of prosperity, which came at length. Just as Jesus was eventually seated at the right hand of God, as Prince and Saviour. And your time, sufferer, shall come at length, when God shall vindicate your character, and avenge your sorrows. "Trust in the Lord, and do good; fret not thyself in any wise to do evil; for evil-doers shall be cut off: but those that wait upon the Lord, they shall inherit the earth. He shall bring forth thy righteousness as the light, and thy judgment as the noonday" (Ps. xxxiv).

II

THE PIT

(GENESIS XXXVII)

"All is of God that is, and is to be;
And God is good! Let this suffice us still;
Resting in childlike trust upon his will,
Who moves to his great ends, unthwarted by the ill."
                                          J. G. WHITTIER.

THE cross of our Lord Jesus Christ is the centre of human history. It is the sun around which the firmament circles; the key to all Scripture history and type; the fact which gives meaning and beauty to all other facts. To ignore the cross is to repeat the error of the old philosophers; who thought that the earth, and not the sun, was the centre of our system, and to whom therefore the very heavens were in confusion. To know and love the cross—to stand beside it as the faithful women did when Jesus died—is to obtain a deep insight into the harmonies of all things in heaven and earth.

It is remarkable to learn that, on the day of our Saviour's passion, it being equinox, the whole habitable world was lit up between the hours of nine a.m. and six p.m. Could an angel have poised himself in mid-air during those memorable hours, he would have seen each continent bathed in successive sunshine. At nine a.m. it was noon in India, and all Asia was in light to its far eastern fringes; at noon all Europe and all Africa was in light; at 6 p.m. the whole continent of America had passed into the golden glory. This may serve as a parable. Poise yourself above the cross; look back to the morning of earth's history, and onward to its evening—and all will be light. The radiance that streams from the cross illumines all events, and banishes all darkness.

When an artist in music, colour, or stone, conceives a beautiful idea, he seems reluctant to let it drop: he hints at it before he expresses it in complete beauty; nor is he satisfied until he has exhausted his art by the variety of ways in which he has embodied his thought. The practised sense may detect it now in the symphony, and then in the chorus; now in the general scheme, and again in the minute detail. It recurs again and again. There is the hint, the outline, the slight symptom, anticipating the fuller, richer revelation. Is not this true also of the death of our beloved Lord? The Great Artist of all things, enamoured with the wondrous cross, filled the world with foreshadowings and anticipations of it long before it stood with outstretched arms on the little hill of Calvary. You may find them in heathen myths, or in ancient sayings and songs. You may find them in touching incidents of human history. You may, above all, find them upon the pages of the Bible. The ages that lie on this side of the cross are full of references to it—it shapes them as it shapes each cathedral church; but I suppose that the ages on the other side were quite as full, though the observers may not have been so keen to see them.

The sun which now shines, so to speak, from the other side of the cross, so as to fling its shadow forward clear and sharp on the canvas of the present, once shone from where we now stand, and flung its shadow backward upon the canvas of the past. One of these shadows is caught and photographed for us in this sweet story of Joseph.

To the casual reader the story of Joseph's wrongs, and of his rise from the pit to vice-regal power, is simply interesting, as an old-world story must ever be, for its archaic simplicity and the insight into the past which it affords. But to the man on whose heart the cross is carved in loving memory there is a far deeper interest. It is Calvary in miniature. It is the outline sketch of the Artist's finished work. It is a rehearsal of the greatest drama ever enacted amongst men.

We can do no better than take it line by line, and mark the fulfilment of the shadow in the glorious reality.

I. JOSEPH'S MISSION.—"*Jacob dwelt in the land* of his father's sojournings." When he had buried his old father he continued to reside in the Vale of Hebron, where Isaac had dwelt for nearly two hundred years, and where Abraham abode before him. This was the headquarters of his vast encampment. But rich as were the pasture-lands of Hebron, they were not sufficient to support the whole of the flocks and herds. The sons were compelled to drive these by slow stages to distant parts of the land; and were even forced, by stern necessity, to brave the anger of the people of Shechem, whom they had grievously wronged, and who had vowed vengeance on them for their foul behaviour.

It was this that gave point to Jacob's question, "Do not thy brethren feed the flock at Shechem?" He had heard them speak of going there in search of pasture; long weeks had passed since he received tidings of their welfare, and the memory of the past made him very anxious about them. And this solicitude became so overpowering that it forced him to do what otherwise would never have entered his thoughts.

He was alone in Hebron with Joseph and Benjamin: they were his darlings; his heart loved them with something of the intense devotion which he had felt towards their mother. Benjamin was young; but Joseph was seventeen years old. The old man kept them with him, reluctant to lose them from his sight. Hebron means fellowship,[1] and was a fitting residence for hearts so closely knit as theirs. But still, on the other hand, the old man yearned with anxious love over his absent sons; and at last, after many battlings and hesitations, he suddenly said to the dearly-loved Joseph, "Come, I will send thee: go, I pray thee, and see whether it be well with thy brethren, and bring me word again."

希伯侖

[1] חֶבְרוֹן *Khevrōn:* Associating, joining together.

On Joseph's part there was not a moment's hesitation. In the flash of a thought he realized the perils of the mission—perils of waters, perils of robbers, perils of wild beasts, perils in the lonely nights, perils among false brethren, who bitterly hated him. But "none of these things moved him, neither counted he his life dear unto himself." As soon as he knew his father's will, he said, "Here am I." "So Jacob sent him; and he came."

But Joseph did not go in search of his brethren simply because his father sent him. Had this been the case, he would have returned home when he found that they had safely left the dreaded Shechem. But instead of that he sought them, because he loved them, and went after them until he found them.

Is not all this full to overflowing of a yet loftier theme? Our Lord never wearied of calling Himself the Sent of the Father. There is hardly a page in the Gospel of John in which He does not say more than once, "I came not of Myself, but My Father sent Me." He loved to find an analogy to His mission in the name of the brooklet that flowed "hard by the oracle of God," and which was called Siloam (which is by interpretation, "Sent"). Thus it became a constant expression with the New Testament writers, "God sent forth his Son"; "The Father sent the Son to be the Saviour of the world."

It must have cost Jacob something to part with the beloved Joseph: and this can be gauged by those who have lost their beloved. But who can estimate how much it cost the Infinite God to send his only-begotten Son, who had dwelt in his bosom, and who was his Fellow from everlasting? Let us not think that God is passionless as the sphinx, which, with expressionless face and with stony eyes, stares unmoved, unfeeling, over the desert waste. If his love be like ours (and we know it must be), He must suffer from the same causes that work havoc in our hearts, only He must suffer proportionately to the strength and infiniteness of his nature. How much, then, must God have loved us, that He should be willing to send his Son! Truly

God *so* loved the world! But who shall fathom the depths of that one small word?

But our Saviour did not come solely because He was sent. He came because He loved his mission. He came to seek and to save that which was lost. And He especially came in search of his brethren, his own, the children of the Hebrew race. Could you have asked Him, as you met Him traversing those same fields, "What seekest Thou?" He would have replied in the self-same words of Joseph, "I seek my brethren." Nor was He content with only *seeking* the lost; He went after them *until* He found them. "Joseph went after his brethren until he found them in Dothan."

Beautiful as is the parable of the Prodigal Son, to me there is a no less priceless beauty in the parables of the Lost Sheep and the Lost Silverling, because in each of these two there was seeking on the part of one who could not bear to lose, and the seeking was never abandoned until the lost was found. It may be that the Lord Jesus is seeking *you*: for many weary days He has been seeking for you, with bleeding feet or with a lighted candle. You of yourself might never have the desire or the courage to seek *Him*; yet take heart, since He will never rest till He has found *you*.

II. JOSEPH'S RECEPTION.—"They saw him afar off, even before he came near unto them, and they conspired against him to slay him." And he would doubtless have been ruthlessly slain, and his body flung into some pit, away from the haunts of men, if it had not been for the merciful pleadings of Reuben, the eldest brother. "And it came to pass, when Joseph was come unto his brethren, that they stripped him of his coat, his coat of many colours, and they took him, and cast him into a pit." Our mother earth has seen many dark crimes committed on her surface by her children; but she has never seen a darker one than this. It was a mean, cowardly, dastardly deed for nine grown men to set upon one timid, unresisting lad.

The calm prose of the historian does not dwell on the passion of the brothers, or on the anguish of that young heart, which found it so hard to die, so hard to say good-bye to the fair earth, so hard to descend into that dark cistern, whose steep sides forbade the hope that he could ever scramble back into the upper air. But the confession of those cruel men, made to one another after the lapse of twenty-five years, enables us to supply the missing colouring for this deed of horror.

Years after they said one to another, "We are verily guilty concerning our brother, in that we saw the anguish of his soul, when he besought us and we would not hear." What a revelation there is in these words! We seem to see Joseph, in those rude hands, like a fleecy lamb in the jaws of a tiger. He struggles to get free. He entreats them with bitter tears to let him go. He implores them for the sake of his old father, and by the tie of brotherhood. The anguish of his soul is clearly evident in his bitter cries, and tears, and prayers. Alas, poor young sufferer! Would that we could believe that thine were the only anguished cries which brutal passion has extorted from gentle innocence!

What a genesis of crime is here! There was a time when the germ of this sin alighted on their hearts in the form of a ruffled feeling of jealousy against the young dreamer. If only they had quenched it then, its further progress would have been stayed. Alas! they did not quench it; they permitted it to work within them as leaven works in meal. And "lust, when it had conceived, brought forth sin; and sin, when it was finished, brought forth death." Take care how you permit a single germ of sin to alight and remain upon your heart. To permit it to do so, is almost certain ruin. Sooner or later it will acquire overwhelming force. Treat that germ as you would the first germ of fever that entered your home. At the first consciousness of sin, seek instant cleansing in the precious blood of Christ.

Unforgiven sin is a fearful scourge. Year passed after year; but the years could not obliterate from their memories that

look, those cries, that scene in the green glen of Dothan, surrounded by the tall cliffs, over-arched by the blue sky, whose
expanse was lit up by a meridian sun. They tried to lock up
the skeleton in their most secret cupboard, but it contrived to
come forth to confront them even in their guarded hours. Sometimes they thought they saw that agonized young face in their
dreams, and heard that piteous voice wailing in the night wind.
The old father, who mourned for his son as dead, was happier
than were they, who knew him to be alive. One crime may
thus darken a whole life. There are some who teach that God
is too merciful to punish men; yet He has so made the world
that sin is its own Nemesis—sin carries with it the seed of its
own punishment. And the men who carry with them the sense
of unforgiven sin, will be the first to believe in a vulture for
ever tearing out the vitals, a worm that never dies, a fire that
is never quenched.

But Joseph's grief was a true anticipation of Christ's. "He
came to his own, but his own received Him not." They said,
"This is the heir, come let us kill Him, and the inheritance shall
be ours." "They caught Him, and cast Him out, and slew
Him." "They parted his raiment among them." They sold
Him to the Gentiles. They sat down to watch Him die. The
anguish of Joseph's soul reminds us of the strong cryings and
tears wrung from the human nature of Christ by the near
approach of His unknown sufferings as the scapegoat of the
race. The comparative innocence of Joseph reminds us of
the spotlessness of the Lamb who was without blemish, and
whose blamelessness was again and again attested before He
died. No victim destined for the altar was ever more search-
ingly inspected for one black hair or defect than was Jesus,
by those who were compelled to confess, "This Man hath
done nothing amiss."

Here, however, the parallel stays. Joseph's sufferings stopped
before they reached the point of death; Jesus tasted death.
Joseph's sufferings were personal; the sufferings of Jesus were
substitutionary and mediatorial; "He died for us"; "He gave

Himself for me." Joseph's sufferings had no efficacy in atoning
for the sin that caused them; but the sufferings of Jesus atone
not only for the guilt of his murderers, but for the guilt of all;
"He is the propitiation for our sins; and not for ours only, but
also for the whole world."

III. JOSEPH'S FATE.—"They sat down to eat bread." With
hardened unconcern they took their midday meal. Just at that
moment a new and welcome sight struck their gaze. They were
sitting on the plain at Dothan, a spot which still retains its
ancient name; and anyone stationed there, and looking eastward towards the valley of the Jordan, would be able to trace
the main road that led from the fords of the Jordan towards
the coast of the Mediterranean. This road was one of the main
thoroughfares of Palestine; it connected Gilead and the other
territories beyond the Jordan with the sea-coast; and when once
the coast was struck, the way was easy southwards through
Philistia to the Delta of the Nile. Along this road at that
moment a caravan was travelling. The brothers could readily
descry the long string of patient camels moving slowly up the
valley towards them. They guessed at once who the parties
were and whence they came. Without doubt they were of the
Arab race, the sailors of the desert in all ages, descendants
of Ishmael; and they were coming from Gilead, bearing
spicery and balm and myrrh, natural aromatic products which
abound in the woods and pasture-lands of Eastern Palestine,
and which were in great request in Egypt for purposes of
embalmment.

The sight of these travelling merchants gave a sudden turn
to the thoughts of the conspirators. They knew that there was
in Egypt a great demand for slaves, and that these merchantmen were in the habit of buying slaves in their passage and
selling them in that land, which has always been the great
slave-mart of the world. Why not sell their brother? It would
be an easy way of disposing of him. It would save them from
fratricide. So, acting upon the suggestion of Judah, they lifted

Joseph out of the pit, and, as money was no object to them, they sold him for twenty rings of silver—about three pounds.

It was the work of a few minutes; and then Joseph found himself one of a long line of fettered slaves, bound for a foreign land. Was not this almost worse than death? What anguish still rent his young heart! How eager his desire to send just one last message to his father! And with all these thoughts, there would mingle a wondering thought of the great God whom he had learned to worship. What would He say to this? Little did he think then that hereafter he should look back on that day as one of the most gracious links in a chain of loving providences; or that he should ever say, "Be not grieved, nor angry with yourselves: God did send me here before you." It is very sweet, as life passes by, to be able to look back on dark and mysterious events, and to trace the hand of God where we once saw only the malice and cruelty of man. And no doubt the day is coming when we shall be able to speak thus of *all* the dark passages of our life.

Joseph was betrayed by his brothers; Jesus by His friend. Joseph was sold for money; so was our Lord. Joseph followed in the train of captives to slavery; Jesus was numbered with transgressors. The crime of Joseph's brothers fulfilled the Divine plan; and the wicked hands of the crucifiers of Jesus fulfilled the determinate counsel and foreknowledge of God.

God will "make the wrath of man to praise Him; and the remainder of wrath will He restrain." "Oh, the depth of the riches both of the wisdom and of the knowledge of God! how unsearchable His judgments, and His ways past finding out!"

III

IN THE HOUSE OF POTIPHAR
(GENESIS XXXIX)

"Many, if God should make them kings,
Might not disgrace the throne He gave;
How few who could as well fulfil
The holier office of a slave!

"Great may he be who can command,
And rule with just and tender sway;
Yet is diviner wisdom taught
Better by him who can obey."
           A. A. PROCTOR.

THE Midianite merchantmen, into whose hands his brethren sold Joseph, brought him down to Egypt—with its riband of green pasture-land amid the waste of sand. In some great slave market he was exposed for sale, together with hundreds more, who had been captured by force or stealth from the surrounding countries. No doubt the regions of the Upper Nile and of Central Africa were drained then as now, to meet the insatiable demand for slaves. And the delicately-complexioned lad may have found himself close to the swarthy children of the lands that lie beneath the tropic sun; lands which have been trodden in recent times by English soldiers, and which will for ever be sacred to our countrymen because of the soldiers' graves that seam the wastes of sand.

He was bought by Potiphar, "the captain of the guard." The margin tells us he was the chief of the slaughtermen or executioners. He was, in all likelihood, the chief of the military force employed as the royal bodyguard, in the precincts of the court. The Egyptian monarchs had the absolute power of life and death; and they did not scruple to order the infliction of a variety of summary or sanguinary punishments, the execution of which was entrusted to the military guard, which was always at hand, and afforded the readiest and most efficient instrument for torture or death.

Potiphar was an Egyptian grandee; a member of a proud aristocracy; high in office and in court favour. He would no doubt live in a splendid palace, covered with hieroglyphs and filled with slaves. The young captive, accustomed to the tendernesses of his simple and beloved home, must have trembled as he passed up the pillared avenue, through sphinx-guarded gates, into the recesses of that strange, vast Egyptian palace, where they spoke a language of which he could not understand a word, and where all was so new and strange. But "God was with him"; the sense of the presence and guardianship of his father's God pervaded and stilled his soul, and kept him in perfect peace; and, though severed from all whom he knew, it was rest and strength to feel that the mysterious wings, engraved on the porticoes of so many Egyptian buildings, were emblems to him of the outstretched wings of his great Father's care—an unsleeping care beneath which his soul might nestle evermore. Who would not rather, after all, choose to be Joseph in Egypt with God, than the brothers with a blood-stained garment in their hands and the sense of guilt on their souls?

Let us consider how Joseph fared in Potiphar's house.

I. JOSEPH'S PROMOTION.—"The Lord was with Joseph; and he was a prosperous man." The older versions of the Bible give a curious rendering here: "The Lord was with Joseph; and he was a luckie fellow." I suppose the meaning is that everything he handled went well. Success followed him as closely as his shadow, and touched all his plans with her magic wand. Potiphar and his household got into the way of expecting that this strange Hebrew captive could untie every knot, disentangle every skein, and bring to successful issues the most intricate arrangements. This arose from two causes.

In the first place, *though stripped of his coat, he had not been stripped of his character*. See to it, young people, that no one rob you of that: everything else may be replaced but that! He was industrious, prompt, diligent, obedient, reliable. When sent to find his brothers, he had carried out, not the letter only, but the spirit of his father's instructions, and did not rest till he had traced them from Shechem to Dothan. And this was the spirit of his life. He did his work, not because he was obliged to do it, but because God had given it to him to do, and had called him to do it. He read the will of God in "the daily round, the common task." He said to himself, as he said in afterlife, "God did send me hither" (xlv. 5). He felt that he was the servant—not so much of Potiphar as—of the God of Abraham and Isaac. There, in the household of Potiphar, he might live a devout and earnest life as truly as when he spent the long, happy days in Jacob's tent: and he did. And it was this which made him so conscientious and careful, qualities which in business must ensure success.

When his fellow-servants were squandering the golden moments, Joseph was filling them with activities. When they were content with a good surface appearance, he toiled upward to success from carefully-laid foundations. When they worked simply to avoid the frown or the lash, he worked to win the smile of the great Taskmaster, whose eye was ever upon him. They often pointed at him with envy, and perhaps said, "He is a lucky fellow." They did not think that his luck was his character; and that his character meant God. Men often speak thus of each other, "He was always a lucky fellow"; "He was born beneath a lucky star"; "He is sure to have good luck." But there is no such thing as luck, except that luck means character. And if you wish to possess such a character as will insure your success in this life, there is no true basis for it but Jesus Christ. You must build on Him; or your structure will be swept away in the first hurricane. But when once you have touched Him, the living stone, with the first courses of faith—then rear the building after the plan given in His own lovely life. Tier on tier let it rise: and you will find that "Godliness is profitable unto all things, and has the promise of the life that now is, and of that which is to come."

In the second place: *"The Lord made all that he did to prosper. The Lord blessed the Egyptian's house for Joseph's sake; and the blessing of the Lord was upon all that he had in the house, and in the field."* This blessing was not the exclusive privilege of Joseph: it is promised to overtake all those "who hearken diligently unto the voice of God, and who observe to do all his commandments" (Deut. xxviii. 1, 2). Such blessing would oft be ours if we walked as near to God as Joseph did. It is of little use to cry with Jabez, "Oh, that Thou wouldest bless me indeed!" unless, like him we add, "Keep me from evil." But when the blessing comes, "it maketh rich, and addeth no sorrow." Let us see to it that we live so that God may be with us. "The Lord is with you, while ye be with Him: and if ye seek Him, He will be found of you; but if ye forsake Him, He will forsake you."

These words may be read by servants of various kinds—the household domestic, the office-boy, the apprentice, the clerk. And if so, they will surely be helped by the example of this noble youth. He did not give himself to useless regrets and unavailing tears. He girded himself manfully to do with his might whatsoever his hand found to do. He was "faithful in that which was least," in the most menial and trivial duties of his office. He believed that God had put him where he was; and in serving his earthly master well he felt that he was really pleasing his great heavenly Friend, who was as near him in those hieroglyphed palaces as in Jacob's tents. This is the spirit in which all service should be done. "Stay where you are," said the apostles to the vast slave populations of their time, who gladly embraced the Gospel that made them free with a freedom which no thongs or chains could limit. But "let every man, wherein he is called, therein abide with God.

Art thou called, being a servant? care not for it; for he that is called in the Lord, being a servant, is the Lord's freeman." "Ye serve the Lord Christ. Whatsoever ye do, do it heartily, as to the Lord, and not unto men." "Be obedient to them that are your masters, in singleness of heart, as unto Christ." "Adorn the doctrine of God our Saviour in all things." "Christ"—the great Servant—"suffered for us, leaving us an example that ye should follow His steps."

These voices from the page of inspiration still speak to servants. If only they were acted upon, all such would as much ask the will of Christ before leaving a situation as a minister before leaving his charge. The most trifling things would be done on the loftiest principles, just as the shape of a dew-drop upon a rose-leaf is determined by the same laws as controlled the moulding of our earth into its present form. Yes: and every kitchen, dwelling-room, and office, would be trodden with the same reverence and love as the floors of a temple or the golden pavement of heaven. Our lots in life are much more even than we think. It is not so important what we do as how we do it. The motive that inspires us is the true gauge and measure of the worth or importance of our life. A mean man may belittle the most momentous affairs by the paltriness of his spirit. A noble man may so greaten trifles by his nobility, that they shall become subjects for the conversation of burning seraphim, or of cherubim with folded wing.

These words may be read by masters. We cannot estimate the worth of a true Christian servant. Happy the household which is thus equipped! The Egyptian Potiphar must have been agreeably surprised at the sudden tide of prosperity which set in towards him. All things went well with him—his cattle throve in the field; his affairs prospered in the house. He may often have questioned the cause, but little guessed at first that it was owing to the Hebrew slave. "The Lord blessed the Egyptian's house for Joseph's sake"; He paid him handsomely for His servant's keep. So is it still. Ungodly masters owe many a blessing to the presence of some Christian servant or *employé* beneath their roof. No angel would ever alight there; no living spring would bubble there; no music would ever sweeten the daily din of work; no ladder would link that building to the skies—if it were not for some Eliezer, or Joseph, or Rhoda, that was living there. When we reach heaven, and are able to trace the origin of things, we shall find that many of the choicest blessings of our lives were procured by the prayers or presence of very obscure and unrecognized people who were dear to God.

II. JOSEPH'S TEMPTATION.—Years passed on, and Joseph became a prosperous man, the steward and bailiff in his master's house. "He left all that he had in Joseph's hand; and he knew not aught he had, save the bread which he did eat." And it was just here that Joseph encountered the most terrible temptation of his life.

We may expect temptation in days of prosperity and ease rather than in those of privation and toil. Not on the glacier slopes of the Alps, but in the sunny plains of the Campagna; not when the youth is climbing arduously the steep ladder of fame, but when he has entered the golden portals; not where men frown, but where they smile sweet exquisite smiles of flattery—it is *there*, it is *there*, that the temptress lies in wait! Beware! If thou goest armed anywhere, thou must, above all, go armed here. Yet this is so hard. It is easy to keep the armour on when we ascend the desolate mountain pass, struggling against the pitiless blast, and afraid that any boulder may hide an assassin. It is hard to keep it buckled close when we have reached the happy valley, with its sultry air. But unless we keep armed there, we are lost. "Watch and pray, that ye enter not into temptation. The flesh is weak."

Temptation is hardest to resist when it arises from the least expected quarter. Egyptian women in those days enjoyed as much liberty as English women do now: this is conclusively proved by the Egyptian monuments, which also testify to the extreme laxity of their morals. It may be that Potiphar's wife was not worse than many of her sex, though we blush to read of her infamous proposals. They must have startled Joseph like a shock of earthquake, and filled him with a sudden tumult of thoughts. The sudden appeal to his passions invested the temptation with tenfold force. God has so arranged it that, for the most part, the sailor is warned against the coming storm; he is able to reef his sails, and close his portholes: but, alas for him if he is caught by a sudden squall! Christian, beware of sudden squalls! Men are suddenly overtaken by faults.

Policy and conscience are often at variance in respect to temptation. It seemed essential to Joseph to stand well with his master's wife. To please her would secure his advancement. To cross her would make her his foe, and ruin his hopes. How many would have reasoned that, by yielding for only a moment, they might win influence which they could afterwards use for the very best results! One act of homage to the devil would invest them with power which they might then use for his overthrow. This is the reasoning of policy, one of the most accursed traitors in man's heart. It is this policy which leads many to say, when tempted to do wrong, by master, or mistress, or foreman, or chief customer, "I did not care for it, or wish it. I yielded because my bread depended on it; I did not dare offend them." The only armour against policy is FAITH that looks to the long future, and believes that in the end it will be found better to have done right, and to have waited the vindication and blessing of God. Well was it for Joseph that he did not heed the suggestions of policy: had he done so, he might have acquired a little more influence in the home of Potiphar; but it could never have lasted—and he would never have become prime minister of Egypt, or had a home of his own, or have brought his boys to receive the blessing of his dying father.

The strength of a temptation lies in the response of our nature to its suggestions. It is said that the germs of the potato and vine disease are always floating in the air; but they can find no place of operation—no bed—in healthy plants. But directly plants become degenerate and unable to resist their attacks, then they sweep away the farmer's hopes in dreadful ruin. So it is with us; if only we were like our Lord, we should pass unscathed through a whirlwind of temptations; they would find nothing in us. It is because our hearts are so desperately wicked that we need to stand in constant watchfulness. "Keep thy heart with all diligence; for out of it are the issues of life." There is no sin in having certain tendencies, appetites, and desires; else there would be sin in hunger, and in drowsiness leading to soft sleep. But the danger lies in the fear that they should be gratified to an immoderate excess, or from wrong and improper sources. Human nature is very liable to this. It is biassed thus; and stolen waters are sweet. Therefore Joseph must have suffered the more.

We should always carefully distinguish between the appetites and desires which are natural to us; and those which we have acquired by evil habit. About the latter we need have no hesitation. We can give them no quarter. They must be cut up root and branch; as weeds from garden soil are thrown upon the bank, that the sun may scorch out their life. But the former need careful watching; because though in themselves they are natural and beautiful, yet they are always liable to demand excessive gratification in respect to right objects, or gratification in directions which are unnatural and forbidden. We must never expect the time to arrive, on this side of death, when these natural tendencies will be rooted out; and so long as they remain in us, they will constitute a *nidus* in which the germs of temptation may sow themselves, and fruit. No thoughtful man, who knows his own weakness, can ever dare to affirm his immunity from temptation, or the impossibility of his yielding. If he stand it is only by the grace of God.

There were peculiar elements of trial in Joseph's case. The temptation was accompanied by opportunity: "there were none of the men there within." It was well timed, and if he had yielded, there was not much fear of detection and punishment; the temptress would never publish her own shame. The temptation was also repeated day by day. How terrible must have been that awful persistency! Water, by constant dropping, will wear away rocks; and the temptation that tries at last to win its way by its very importunity is to be feared most of all.

Yet Joseph stood firm. He reasoned with her. He urged his master's kindness and trust. He held up the confidence which he dared not betray. He tried to recall her to a sense of what became her as his master's wife. But he did more. He brought the case from the court of reason to that of conscience, and asked in words for ever memorable, and which have given the secret of victory to tempted souls in all ages: "How shall I do this great wickedness, and sin against God!"

There are few subjects which require more notice both from speakers and writers than this great subject of chastity. Society is merciless on the occasional consequences of unchastity and on the wretched victims; but it hears of the sin itself with an averted smile, or calls it by some other name. But there is no one sin which sooner corrupts the heart, weakens the intellect, and destroys the body. The poet Robert Burns wrote out of a bitter experience in his "Letter to a Young Friend":

> "*The hallowed lowe o' weel-placed love,*
>   *Luxuriantly indulge it;*
> *But never tempt the illicit rove,*
>   *Though naething should divulge it.*
> *I waive the quantum o' the sin,*
>   *The hazard o' concealin';*
> *But oh, it hardens a' within,*
>   *And petrifies the feelin'.*"

And Lord Byron, ending his brief and unchaste life at the age of thirty-six, closed his last poem with these mournful words:

"My days are in the yellow leaf,
The flower and fruit of love are gone:
The worm, the canker, and the grief,
Are mine alone!"

There is no one sin which will sooner bring about a nation's fall. If history teaches anything, it teaches that sensual indulgence is the surest way to national ruin. Society in not condemning this sin condemns herself.

It is said that the temptations of our great cities are too many and strong for the young to resist. Men sometimes speak as if sin were a necessity. Refuse to entertain such thoughtlessness and dangerous talk. Whilst the case of Joseph remains on record, it is a standing contradiction to the whole. A young man *can* resist; he *can* overcome; he *can* be pure, and chaste, and sweet. We must, however, obey the dictates of Scripture and common sense. Avoid all places, books, and people which minister to evil thoughts. Resist the first tiny rill of temptation, lest it widen a breach big enough to admit the ocean. Remember that no temptation can master you unless you admit it *within* your nature; and since you are too weak to keep the door shut against it, look to the mighty Saviour to place Himself against it. All hell cannot break the door open which you entrust to the safe keeping of Jesus.

What a motto this is for us all! "How can *I* do this great wickedness?" *I*, for whom Christ died. "How can I do this great *wickedness*?" Others call it "gaiety"; "being a little fast"; "sowing wild oats." I call it SIN. "How can I do this *great* wickedness?" Many wink at it; to me it is a *great* sin. "How can I sin *against God*?" It seems only to concern men; but in effect it is a personal sin against the holy God.

It might have been better if Joseph had not gone into the house to do his business; but probably he had no choice except to go. He took care not to be with her (ver. 10) more than he could help. We have no right to expect God to keep us if we voluntarily put ourselves into temptation. But if we are compelled to go there by the circumstances of our life, we may count upon His faithfulness. If the Spirit driveth us into the wilderness to be tempted, we may expect to enjoy also the ministry of the angels.

Joseph did a wise thing when he fled. Discretion is often the wisest part of valour. Better lose a coat and many a more valuable possession than lose a good conscience. "Flee youthful lusts." Do not parley with temptation. Do not linger in its vicinity. Do not stay to look at it. It will master you if you do. "Escape for thy life; look not behind thee, neither stay in all the plain."

There is no sin in being tempted. The Sinless One Himself was tempted of the devil. The mob may batter at the palace gates; but the national life is safe so long as sin does not penetrate into the throne-room, and thrust itself into the royal seat. The will is the citadel of our manhood; and so long as there is no yielding there, there is none anywhere. I cannot be accused of receiving stolen goods, if I am simply asked to take them in—a request which I indignantly repudiate. The sin comes in when I assent, and acquiesce, and yield. At the same time, it is in the highest degree unwise to relinquish the battle until it comes into the inner shrine of our being. Much better fight it in the first circle of defence—in the first suggestion, or insinuation, or desire. Resist the devil there, and he will flee from you; and you will be saved a struggle within, which will leave its scar on your soul for years to come.

May we have grace and faith to imitate the example of Joseph, and, above all, of our stainless Lord. We may be quite sure that no temptation will be permitted to assail us—but such as is common to man, or that we are able to resist. The onset of temptation indicates that God knows that we are strong enough to resist, and that sufficient grace is surely within our reach. And the Almighty Father would lead us to put forth that strength, and to avail ourselves of His resources. "He that abideth in Him sinneth not. He that sinneth hath not seen Him, neither known Him." Never forget that we who believe in Jesus are seated with Him at the right hand of power; nor that Satan is already, in the purpose of God, a defeated foe beneath our feet. Let the Overcomer into your heart, for Him to overcome in you, as He overcame in His own mortal life (1 John iv. 4; and John xvi. 33). Open your whole being to the subduing grace of the Holy Spirit. And thus we shall be more than conquerors through Him who loves us.

IV

THE SECRET OF PURITY

(GENESIS XXXIX. *See also* Prov. iv. 23; 1 Pet. i. 5; 2 Tim. i. 12)

> *"Against the threats of malice, or of sorcery, or that power*
> *Which erring men call Chance, this I hold firm:*
> *Virtue may be assailed, but never hurt;*
> *Surprised by unjust force, but not enthralled;*
> *Yea, even that which mischief meant most harm,*
> *Shall, in the happy trial, prove most glory."*
>
> MILTON.

JOSEPH learnt, hundreds of years before our Saviour taught it from the Mount of the Beatitudes, the blessedness of the pure in heart. He could not have anticipated the exquisite symmetry of the form in which the law of that blessedness was expressed. That could only be coined and minted by the lips which spake as never man spake. But he most certainly drank a deep draught of divine sweetness and light from the crystal vase of his manly purity.

There is nothing which we more earnestly admire than purity, like that which Milton, our great Puritan bard, so exquisitely paints in his "Comus"; and which, like the sunbeam striking through the atmosphere of some fœtid court, can pass through the murkiest conditions, without surrendering a ray of its celestial glory. Men familiar with the secret of self-control —or who, not having been exposed to the gusts of temptations which sweep over and master other lives, have never sullied their robes—always attract to themselves the admiration and reverence of their fellows. The snow-capt summits of purity, in their lofty, heaven-reaching majesty, appear so inaccessible to ordinary men, that they wonder greatly at any who are able to scale their rugged sides and breathe the rare atmosphere of the heavenly world.

We must always bear in mind that there is no part of our nature, no function of our human life, which is in itself common or unclean. As Adam came from his Maker's hand, and stood before Him in his native innocence, he did not even need the fig-leaf drapery. All was sweet, and pure, and right, and very good. There was no desire or appetite of his nature which in itself was less sacred than any other. And if only he had ever willed God's will—if only the will, and law, and purpose of God had been kept supreme in his inner economy—there had been no lust, no inordinate desire, no passion, in the world. Like Moses, the great lawgiver, on the wilderness march, who received the commands of God and handed them to the officers and elders for the obedience of the host, so could conscience have received from God, and transmitted to the entire economy of our human nature, those enactments, the legitimate out-working of which had been towards the glory of God on the one hand, and man's well-being on the other.

But when man sinned in the glades of Paradise, he changed the pivot of his being from God to self; he loved and served the creature more than the Creator; he took the sun out of the centre of the inner sphere, which immediately fell into confusion, each part working for its own selfish and immediate gratification. And from that time man's highest law has consisted in the indulgence of appetite, flinging the reins on the neck of inordinate desire, whether of gross physical indulgence, or of imagination and thought; the only restraint being imposed by the fear of disastrous consequences in name or position; in mind, body, or estate.

This fact must be borne in mind then, in considering ourselves or others; and we must take into account the operation of the great law of heredity, by which we have become possessed of appetites and tendencies, which, however pure in their original intention, have been vitiated through the abuse of the many generations from which we have sprung. And there is, therefore, a strong tendency in us all by nature towards the forbidden fruit. Who amongst us has not been often conscious of a bias towards selfish indulgence in two distinct ways: first, to gratify the senses in directions which are wholly forbidden; and next, to gratify them to an excessive extent in directions which are in themselves legitimate?

It is inevitable, therefore, that we should begin life under serious disadvantages, since by our very origin we are closely related to a race which, through ages of previous history, has been tainted by the poison of self-will, and swept by the storms of passion. We cannot but start under serious disadvantages as compared with Adam. Not that we are condemned for his sin, for we are told that the second Adam has met for us all those penal consequences which must otherwise have accrued to us on that account; but that we are terribly handicapped by the disadvantage of being the children of a fallen race. And is not this what is meant by the theological term, *original sin*; and by St. Paul's phrase, "the law in the members"? And if it should be alleged that some mysterious change has passed over our physical nature, by which the inherited morbid opera-tion of natural appetite has been reversed, we ask for proof and Scriptural warrant. Certainly, the presence of disease in the bodies of some of the holiest people is a strong presumptive proof against any such change having been effected. We must either hold that we have already received the resurrection-body, or that there are perverted natural tendencies towards unholy and selfish gratification.

To guard against all possible misconstruction, we reiterate that we do not hold sin to consist in a merely physical state or act; but that we are predisposed to sin by the very nature which we have inherited, and which is so susceptive of Satanic temptation on the one side, and so subtle, swift, and disastrous in its influence on the will upon the other: and no philosophy of the inner life can be satisfactory that does not recognize the presence of this body of flesh, which is not in itself sin, but which so readily lends itself to evil suggestion, that, falling on it as sparks on gunpowder, tends to inflame the imagination, heart, and will.

So long, therefore, as we are in the body, we cannot say that we stand where Adam stood when he first came from the moulding hand of God. There is a great difference between us and him, in that at that moment his nature had never yet yielded to evil; whilst ours has done so thousands of times, both in those from whom we have received it, and in our own repeated acts of self-indulgence. The glad time is coming when we shall exchange this body of humiliation for one in the likeness of our Saviour's Resurrection. Then one great source of temptation and failure will be removed, and we shall no longer have to complain that the law in our members wars against the law of our mind, with the design of bringing us into its fatal captivity.

Is there then no deliverance in this life from that bondage? Surely there is. The law in the members may war against the law of the mind, and yet not succeed in bringing it into captivity, because it shall be garrisoned and held by the law of the Spirit of Life, which is in Christ Jesus, and which makes free from the law of sin and death.

The one-sufficient power by which the promptings of our evil nature can be held in check is by the indwelling and infilling of the Holy Spirit. "Walk in the Spirit, and ye shall not fulfil the lust of the flesh. The flesh lusteth against the Spirit, and the Spirit against the flesh, that ye may not do the things that ye would."

Never in this life will the tempter cease to assail. Even in the heavenly places—the upper regions of spiritual experience—we shall still be exposed to the attacks of the hosts of wicked spirits; and so long as we tabernacle in this body, we shall carry with us that susceptibility to evil which is the bitter result of Adam's fall. Like a thrill of electricity which pervades in a single moment the entire range of a telegraphic system, so some flash of unholy suggestion may rush through our nature, causing it for a moment to vibrate and thrill.

But when the Holy Spirit fills us, the tempter may do his worst, and his suggestions will fall fruitless and ineffectual at our feet; our nature will not respond to the solicitations which are made to it from without. We all know what happens when matches are struck on damp surfaces; and it will be thus with our temptations. The old nature, which was once as inflammable as gunpowder, will be deprived, so to speak, so long as the Spirit is in possession, of its terrible facility of response. And even more, when the Spirit is in mighty power within, He will take away the very desire to yield to sin, and change the old love into hate, so that we shall loathe and shudder at things which we formerly chose and revelled in.

And in many cases, where He is trusted to the uttermost, He does his work so quietly and effectually in keeping the sinful tendencies in the place of death, that the happy subject of His grace supposes that they have been extracted from the nature. They are as if they were not. The self-life seems to hibernate; and this blessed experience continues, just so long as the soul lives in the full enjoyment of the Blessed Spirit's work.

Would that it might be the happy portion of each reader of these lines!

V

Misunderstood and Imprisoned[1]
(Genesis xxxix, xl. *See also* Ps. cv. 17–19)

"Choose for us, Lord, nor let our weak preferring
Cheat us of good Thou hast for us designed:
Choose for us, Lord; Thy wisdom is unerring,
And we are fools and blind.

"Let us press on, in patient self-denial,
Accept the hardship, shrink not from the loss:
Our portion lies beyond the hour of trial,
Our crown beyond the cross."
                                            W. H. BURLEIGH.

BETWEEN the pit and the prison there was only a transient gleam of sunlight and prosperity. The sky of Joseph's life was again soon overcast. For when Potiphar heard the false but plausible statement of his wife, and saw the garment in her hand, which he recognized as Joseph's, his wrath flamed up; he would hear no words of explanation, but thrust him at once into the state prison, of which he had the oversight and charge.

I. THE SEVERITY OF HIS SUFFERINGS.—It was not a prison like those with which we are familiar—airy, well-lit, and conducted by humane men. To use Joseph's own words, in the Hebrew, it was a miserable "hole."[2] "I have done nothing that they should put me into the 'hole.'" We are reminded of the words, describing old Bedford prison, with which Bunyan

---

[1] Some thoughts in this chapter were suggested by an article in the "Expositor's Notebook" by Rev. S. Cox.
[2] בּוֹר—*Bōr.*

commences his matchless allegory: "As I walked through the wilderness of this world, I lighted on a certain place where was a den, and I laid me down in that place to sleep; and, as I slept, I dreamed a dream." Two or three little rooms, crowded with prisoners, stifling in air, fœtid with ill odours, perhaps half-buried from the blessed sunshine—this was the sort of accommodation in which Joseph spent those two miserable years.

Those who have seen the dreary prison at Tangier will be able to form a better conception of what that "hole" must have been like. Imagine a large gloomy hall, with no windows, paved with flags black with filth, no light or air, save what may struggle through the narrow grated aperture, by which the friends of the wretched inmates, or some pitying strangers, pass in the food and water which are the sole staff of life: no arrangements of any kind being made for cleanliness, or for the separation of the prisoners. All day long there is the weary clank of fetters round manacled feet, as the victims slowly drag themselves over the floor, or revolve again and again around the huge stone columns which support the roof, and to which their chains are riveted. In more ways than one does the Gospel of Christ preach deliverance to the captives. In some such sunless "hole" must Joseph have been confined.

And this was hard enough for one who was wont to wander freely on the broad Syrian plains. Confinement is intolerable to us all, but especially to youth, and of all youth most so to those in whose veins flows something of that Arab blood which dreads death less than bondage. I do not wonder at the pathetic story which tells how, on London Bridge, a sunburnt sailor, fresh from the docks, bought cage after cage of imprisoned wild birds, and let them fly rejoicing to their native woods, assigning as his reason to the wondering on-lookers that he had languished too long in a foreign prison not to know how sweet freedom was. We do not realize how priceless freedom is, because we have never lost it. And Joseph never valued it as he did when he found himself shut up in that stifling "hole".

But in addition to the confinement of the prison, *there was the constant clank of the fetter.* He was bound, and his feet were hurt by fetters. True, he enjoyed the favour of the keeper of the prison, and had exceptional liberty within the gloomy precincts so as to reach the inmates; but still, wherever he moved, the rattle of the iron reminded him that he was a prisoner still. You remember a touching allusion of another of the Lord's prisoners to this self-same thing. So Paul took from the hand of his amanuensis the pen with which to write his autograph, "the token in every epistle" of genuineness and authenticity; and as he did so, he felt the pull of the chain that fastened him to the soldier of the imperial guard; and we can almost hear the clanking of the iron in the words, "Remember my bonds" (Col. iv. 18).

But besides all this, *his religious notions added greatly to his distress.* He had been taught by Jacob the theory which comes out so prominently in the speeches of Job's three friends, and which was so generally held by all their teachers and associates in that olden, Eastern, philosophic, deeply-pondering world: that good would come to the good, and evil to the bad; that prosperity was the sign of the Divine favour, and adversity of the Divine anger. And Joseph had tried to be good. Had he not always kept his father's commandments and acted righteously, though his brethren were men of evil report, and tried to make him as bad as themselves? But what had he gained by his integrity? Simply the murderous jealousy and hatred of his own flesh and blood. Had he not, in the full flush of youthful passion, resisted the blandishments of the beautiful Egyptian, because he would not sin against God? And what had he gained by that? Simply the stigma which threatened to cling to him of having committed the very wickedness it was so hard not to commit; and, in addition, an undeserved punishment. Had he not always been kind and gentle to his fellow-prisoners, listening to their stories, speaking comfort to their hearts? And what had he gained by that? To judge by what he saw, simply nothing; and he might as well have kept his kindness to himself.

Was it of any use, then, being good? Could there be any truth in what his father had taught him of good coming to the good, and evil to the bad? Was there a God who judgeth righteously in the earth? You who have been misunderstood, who have sown seeds of holiness and love to reap nothing but disappointment, loss, suffering, and hate—*you* know something of what Joseph felt in that wretched dungeon hole.

Then, too, disappointment poured her bitter drops into the bitter cup. What had become of those early dreams, those dreams of coming greatness, which had filled his young brain with splendid phantasmagoria? Were these not from God? He had thought so—yes, and his venerable father had thought so too; and *he* should have known, for he had talked with God many a time. Were those imaginings the delusions of a fevered brain, or mocking lies? Was there no truth, no fidelity, in heaven or earth? Had God forsaken him? Had his father forgotten him? Did his brothers ever think of him? Would they ever try and find him? Was he to spend all his days in that dungeon, dragging on a weary life, never again enjoying the bliss of freedom: and all because he had dared to do right? Do you wonder at the young heart being weighed almost to breaking?

And yet Joseph's experience is not alone. You may have never been confined in a dungeon; and yet you may have often sat in darkness, and felt around you the limitation which forbade your doing as you wished. You may have been doing right, and doing right may have brought you into some unforeseen difficulty; and you are disposed to say, "I have been too honest." Or you may have been doing a noble act to someone, as Joseph did to Potiphar, and it has been taken in quite a wrong light. Who does not know what it is to be misunderstood, misrepresented, accused falsely, and punished wrongfully?

Each begins life so buoyantly and hopefully. Youth, attempting the solution of the strange problem of existence, fears nothing, forbodes no ill. The minstrel, Hope, keys her chords to the loftiest strains of exultation. The sun shines; the blue wavelets break in music around the boat; the sails swell gently; Love and Beauty hold the rudder-bands; and though stories of the wreckage of the treacherous sea are freely told, there is no kind of fear that such experiences should ever overtake that craft. But presently disappointment, sorrow, and disaster over-cloud the sky and blot out the sunny prospect; and the young mariner wakes as from a dream, "Can this be I, who imagined that I should never see ill?" Then come several tremendous struggles of the soul to wrench itself free. The muscles are strained as whipcord; the beads of perspiration stand on the brow: but every effort only entangles the limbs more helplessly. And at last, exhausted and helpless, the young life ceases to struggle, and lies still, cowed and beaten, as the wild denizen of the plains, when it has lain for hours in the hunter's snare. Surely there was something of this sort in Joseph's condition, as he lay in that wretched dungeon.

II. THESE SUFFERINGS WROUGHT VERY BENEFICIALLY.— Taken on the lowest ground, *this imprisonment served Joseph's temporal interests.* That prison was the place where state prisoners were bound. Thither court magnates who had fallen under suspicion were sent. Chief butler and chief baker do not seem much to us, but they were titles for very august people. Such men would talk freely with Joseph; and in doing so would give him a great insight into political parties, and a knowledge of men and things generally, which in after-days must have been of great service to him.

But there is more than this. Psalm cv. 18, referring to Joseph's imprisonment, has a striking alternative rendering, "His soul entered into iron." Turn that about, and render it in our language, and it reads thus, *Iron entered into his soul.* Is there not a truth in this? It may not be the truth intended in that verse, but it is a very profound truth, that sorrow and privation, the yoke borne in the youth, the soul's enforced restraint, are all conducive to an iron tenacity and strength of purpose, an endurance, a fortitude, which are the indispensable foundation and framework of a noble character. Do not flinch from suffering. Bear it silently, patiently, resignedly; and be assured that it is God's way of infusing iron into your spiritual make-up.

As a boy, Joseph's character tended to softness. He was a little spoilt by his father. He was too proud of his coat. He was rather given to tell tales. He was too full of his dreams and foreshadowed greatness. None of these were great faults; but he lacked strength, grip, power to rule. But what a difference his imprisonment made in him! From that moment he carries himself with a wisdom, modesty, courage, and manly resolution, that never fail him. He acts as a born ruler of men. He carries an alien country through the stress of a great famine, without a symptom of revolt. He holds his own with the proudest aristocracy of the time. He promotes the most radical changes. He had learned to hold his peace and wait. Surely the iron had entered his soul!

It is just this that suffering will do for you. The world wants iron dukes, iron battalions, iron sinews, and thews of steel. God wants iron saints; and since there is no way of imparting iron to the moral nature than by letting his people suffer, He lets them suffer. "No chastening for the present seemeth to be joyous, but grievous; nevertheless afterward it yieldeth the peaceable fruit of righteousness unto them which are exercised thereby." Are you in prison for doing right? Are the best years of your life slipping away in enforced monotony? Are you beset by opposition, misunderstanding, obloquy, and scorn, as the thick undergrowth besets the passage of the woodsman pioneer? Then take heart; the time is not wasted; God is only putting you through the iron regimen. The iron crown of suffering precedes the golden crown of glory. And iron is entering into your soul to make it strong and brave.

Is some aged eye perusing these words? If so, the question may be asked, Why does God sometimes fill a whole life with discipline, and give few opportunities for showing the iron

quality of the soul? Why give iron to the soul, and then keep
it from active service? Ah, that is a question which goes far
to prove our glorious destiny. There must be another world
somewhere, a world of glorious ministry, for which we are
training. "There is service in the sky." And it may be that
God counts a human life of seventy years of suffering not too
long an education for a soul which may serve Him through
the eternities. It is in the prison that Joseph is fitted for the
unknown life of Pharaoh's palace; and if he could have fore-
seen the future, he would not have wondered at the severe
discipline. If only we could see all that awaits us in the palace
of the Great King, we should not be so surprised at certain
experiences which befall us in earth's darker cells. You are
being trained for service in God's Home, and in the upper
spaces of his universe.

III. JOSEPH'S COMFORT IN THE MIDST OF THESE SUFFER-
INGS.—"He was there in the prison; *but the Lord was with
him.*" The Lord was with him in the palace of Potiphar;
but when Joseph went to prison, the Lord went there too.
The only thing which severs us from God is sin: so long
as we walk with God, God will walk with us; and if our path
dips down from the sunny upland lawns into the valley with
its clinging mists, He will go at our side. The godly man is
much more independent of men and things than others. It is
God who makes him blessed. Like the golden city, he has no
need of sun or moon, for the Lord God is his everlasting light.
If he is in a palace he is glad, not so much because of its delights
as because God is there. And if he is in a prison he can sing
and give praises, because the God of his love bears him company. To the soul which is absorbed with God, all places and
experiences are much the same. "If I say, Surely the darkness
shall cover me; even the night [of sorrow and of confinement]
shall be light about me: yea, the night shineth as the day."

Moreover, *the Lord showed him mercy.* Oh, wondrous revelation! He did not stand in a niche on the mountainside, as

Moses did, whilst the solemn pomp swept past; and yet the Lord showed him a great sight—He showed him his mercy. That prison-cell was the mount of vision, from the height of which he saw, as he had never seen before, the panorama of Divine loving kindness. It were well worth his while to go to prison to learn that. When children gather to see the magic lantern, the figures may be flung upon the sheet, and yet be invisible, because the room is full of light. Darken the room, and instantly the round circle of light is filled with brilliant colour. God our Father has often to turn down the lights of our life because He wants to show us mercy. Whenever you get into a prison of circumstances, be on the watch. Prisons are rare places for seeing things. It was in prison that Bunyan saw his wondrous allegory, and Paul met the Lord, and John looked through heaven's open door, and Joseph saw God's mercy. God has no chance to show his mercy to some of us except when we are in some sore sorrow. The night is the time to see the stars.

God can also raise up friends for his servants in most unlikely places, and of most unlikely people. "The Lord gave him favour in the sight of the keeper of the prison." He was probably a rough, unkindly man, quite prepared to copy the dislikes of his master, the great Potiphar, and to embitter the daily existence of this Hebrew slave. But there was another Power at work, of which he knew nothing, inclining him towards his ward, and leading him to put him in a position of trust. All hearts are open to our King: at his girdle swing the keys by which the most unlikely door can be unlocked. "When a man's ways please the Lord, He maketh even his enemies to be at peace with him." It is as easy for God to turn a man's heart, as it is for the husbandman to turn the course of a brook to carry fertility to an arid plot.

There is always alleviation for our troubles in ministry to others. Joseph found it so. It must have been a welcome relief to the monotony of his grief when he found himself entrusted with the care of the royal prisoners. A new interest came into his life, and he almost forgot the heavy pressure of his own troubles amid the interest of listening to the tales of those who were more unfortunate than himself. It is very interesting to notice what a deep human interest he took in the separate cases of his charges, noticing the expression of their faces, inquiring kindly after their welfare, sitting down to listen to their tale. Joseph is the patron of all prison philanthropists; but he took to this holy work not primarily because he had an enthusiasm for it, but because it gave a welcome opiate to his own griefs.

There is no anodyne for heart-sorrow like ministry to others. If your life is woven with the dark shades of sorrow, do not sit down to deplore in solitude your hapless lot, but arise to seek out those who are more miserable than you are, bearing them balm for their wounds and love for their heart-breaks. And if you are unable to give much practical help, you need not abandon yourself to the gratification of lonely sorrow, for you may largely help the children of bitterness by imitating Joseph in listening to their tales of woe or to their dreams of foreboding. It is a great art to be a good listener. The burdened heart longs to pour out its tale in a sympathetic ear. There is immense relief in the telling out of pain. But it cannot be hurried; it needs plenty of time; it cannot clear itself of its silt and deposits unless it is allowed leisure to stand. And so the sorrowful turn away from men engaged in the full rush of active life as too busy, and seek out those who, like themselves, have been "winged," and are obliged to go softly, as Joseph was, when the servants of Pharaoh found him in the Egyptian dungeon. If you can do nothing else, listen well, and comfort others with the comfort wherewith you yourself have been comforted by God.

And as you listen, and comfort, and wipe the falling tears, you will discover that your own load is lighter, and that a branch or twig of the true tree—the tree of the Cross—has fallen into the bitter waters of your own life, making the Marah, Naomi, and the marshes of salt tears will have been

healed. Out of such intercourse you will get what Joseph got—
the key which will unlock the heavy doors by which you have
been shut in.

*And now some closing words to those who are suffering
wrongfully. Do not be surprised.* You are the followers of One
who was misunderstood from the age of twelve to the day of
his ascension; who did not sin, and yet was counted as a
sinner; concerning whom the unanimous testimony was, "I
find in Him no fault at all"; and yet they called Him Beelze-
bub! If they spoke thus of the Master of the house, how much
more concerning the household! "Think it not strange concerning the fiery trial that is to try you, as though some strange
thing happened unto you"; only be sure that you suffer wrongfully, and as a Christian.

Do not get weary in well-doing. Joseph might have said, "I
give all up; of what profit is my godliness? I may as well live
as others do." How much nobler was his course of patient
continuance in well-doing! Do right, because it is right to do
right; because God sees you; because it puts gladness into the
heart. And then, when you are misunderstood and ill-treated,
you will not swerve, or sit down to whine and despair.

Above all, do not avenge yourselves. When Joseph recounted
his troubles, he did not recriminate harshly on his brethren, or
Potiphar, or Potiphar's wife. He simply said: "I was stolen
away out of the land of the Hebrews, and here also have I done
nothing that they should put me into the hole." He might have
read the words of the apostle, "Avenge not yourselves, but
rather give place unto wrath." "If when ye do well, and
suffer for it, ye take it patiently, this is acceptable with God."
We make a great mistake in trying always to clear ourselves;
we should be much wiser to go straight on, humbly doing the
next thing, and leaving God to vindicate us. "He will bring
forth our righteousness as the light, and our judgment as the
noonday." In Psalm cv. 19 there follow words which, rightly
rendered, read thus: "The word of the Lord cleared him."
What a triumphant clearing did God give His faithful servant!

There will come hours in all our lives, when we shall be misconstrued, misunderstood, slandered, falsely accused, wrongfully persecuted. At such times it is very difficult not to act on the policy of the men around us in the world. They at once appeal to law and force and public opinion. But the believer takes his case into a higher court, and lays it before his God. He is prepared to use any means that may appear divinely suggested. But he relies much more on the divine clearing than he does on his own most perfect arrangements. He is content to wait for months and years, till God arise to avenge his cause. It is a very little thing for him to be judged adversely at the bar of man: he cares only for the judgment of God, and awaits the moment when the righteous shall shine forth in the kingdom of their Father, as the sun when it breaks from all obscuring mists. "When Christ, who is our life, shall be manifested, then shall ye also with Him be manifested in glory." Ah! what a clearing-up of mysteries, what dissipating of misunderstandings, what vindication of character shall be there! Oh, slandered ones, you can afford to await the verdict of eternity; of God, who will bring out your righteousness as the light, and your judgment as the noonday.

In all the discipline of life it is of the utmost importance to see but one ordaining overruling will. If we view our imprisonments and misfortunes as the result of human malevolence, our lives will be filled with fret and unrest. It is hard to suffer wrong at the hands of man, and to think that perhaps it might have never been. But there is a truer and more restful view, to consider all things as being under the law and rule of God; so that though they may originate in and come to us through the spite and malice of our fellows, yet, since before they reach us they have had to pass through the environing atmosphere of the Divine Presence, they have been transformed into his own sweet will for us.

It was Judas who plotted our Saviour's death, and filled the garden with the capturing bands and flashing lights; and yet the Lord Jesus said that the Father was putting the cup to his lips. And though He was murdered by the chief priests and scribes, yet He so thoroughly acquiesced in the Father's appointment, that He spoke of *laying down* his life, as if his death were entirely his own act. There is no evil to them that love God; and the believer loses sight of second causes, so absorbed is he in the contemplation of the unfolding of the mystery of his Father's will. As the dying Kingsley said, "All is under law."

We must not be surprised when dark passages come in our outward life, or our inner experience. Unbroken sunshine would madden our brains; and unsullied prosperity of soul or circumstance would induce a spiritual excitement, which would be in the last degree deleterious. We must be sometimes deprived of feeling, that we may acquire the art of walking by faith. We must lose the supporting cork belt that we may be compelled to trust ourselves to the buoyant wave. We must descend into the darksome glen, that we may test for ourselves the reliability of the staff and the rod, which before we may have considered as superfluities or as ornaments.

> *He sent a man before them,*
>> *Even Joseph, who was sold for a servant,*
> *Whose feet they hurt with fetters;*
>> *He was laid in iron,*
> *Until the time that His word came:*
>> *The word of the Lord tried him.*
> *The king sent and loosed him,*
>> *Even the ruler of the people,*
>> *And let him go free.*
> *He made him lord of his house,*
>> *And ruler of all his substance;*
> *To bind his princes at his pleasure,*
> *And teach his senators wisdom.*

PSALM CV. 17–22.

VI

THE STEPS OF THE THRONE
(GENESIS XLI)

"The heights by great men reached and kept
Were not obtained by sudden flight;
But they, while their companions slept,
Were toiling upward in the night.

"Standing on what too long we bore,
With shoulders bent and downcast eyes,
We may discern—unseen before—
A path to higher destinies!"
                                        LONGFELLOW.

THE facts of Joseph's exaltation from the prison-cell in which we left him, to the steps of Pharaoh's throne, are so well known that we need not describe them in detail. We will dwell briefly on the more salient points.

I. HOPE DEFERRED.—"Remember me when it shall be well with thee." It was a modest and pathetic prayer that Joseph made to the great officer of state, to whose dream he had given so favourable an interpretation. Some, however, have said he had no right to make it. They have said that he had no right to ask this man to plead with Pharaoh, when he himself had access to the King of kings, and could at all times plead his case at his court. The Moslem thought embodies itself in a characteristic legend. It says that God had changed his cell into a pleasant and cheerful place by causing a fountain to spring up in the midst, and a tree to grow at the door with shadowing branches and luscious fruit: but that, when he made this request to the chief butler, the fountain fell down and the tree withered; and this because, instead of trusting in God, he had relied on the help of a feeble man.

Well, there may be some truth at the foundation of all this; and yet it ill becomes us to bear hardly on the captive in the hour of his soul's deepest anguish. The strongest faith has wavered at times. Elijah sank down on the desert sand, and asked that he might die. John the Baptist, daunted and despondent, sent from his gloomy cell in Herod's castle to know if Jesus were indeed the Christ. Savonarola, Luther, Edward Irving, passed through darkness so thick that it almost put out the torch of their heroic faith; and if at this moment Joseph eagerly snatched at human help, as being nearer and more real than the help of God, who of us can condemn him? who of us can help sympathizing with him? who of us would not have behaved in like manner? Many a time when we have professed that our soul waited only upon God, we have either eagerly hinted at or openly shown our needs to those whom we thought likely to assist.

This cry, "Remember me," reminds us of the prayer of the dying thief to our Lord, as he was entering into the thick darkness. But how different the reply! The promise was quickly made and swiftly kept. And as the sun was setting over the western hills, the believing penitent had entered the city which is never bathed in sunset glory, and had learnt what it is to be in Paradise with Christ. Far otherwise it was with Joseph.

The great man no doubt readily acceded to his request, and promised all he asked. "Remember you," he said; "of course I will." And, doubtless, in the fulness of his heart, he resolved to give Joseph a place among the under-butlers, or perhaps in the vineries. And as he passed out, we can imagine him saying, "Good-bye: you will hear from me soon." But he "forgat". Oh, that word "forgat"! How many of us know what it means! Day after day, as Joseph went about his duties, he expected to receive some token of his friend's remembrance and intercession. Week after week he watched for the message of deliverance, and often started because of some sudden knock which made him think that the warrant for his release had come. Then he invented ingenious excuses for the delay. No doubt the butler had had to receive the congratulations of his friends; arrears of business had perhaps accumulated in his absence, and now engrossed his attention; many things had probably gone wrong which required time and pains to set right; or perhaps he was waiting for a good opportunity to urge the claims of his prison friend on the king. How many hours of anxious thought were spent thus, hoping against hope, combating a sickly fear, which he hardly dared to entertain! But at last it was useless to hide from himself the unpalatable truth, which slowly forced itself upon his mind, that he was forgotten.

Hope deferred must have made his heart sick. But he kept steadfast. If he was disappointed in man, he clung the more tenaciously to God. "My soul," said he, in effect, "wait thou only upon God; for my expectation is from Him. He only is my rock and my salvation." Nor did he trust in vain; for, by a chain of wonderful providences, God brought him out of prison, and did better for him than could have been done by the chief butler of Pharaoh's court.

It may be that some who read these lines are in perplexity or distress which may be compared to that of Joseph when in the dungeon. And they have again and again schemed to effect their own deliverance. They helped a friend to emigrate, on the understanding that, if he got on well, he should send money to help them over too. They have applied to people who were befriended by them when they lived in the same poor street, but who have subsequently risen greatly in the world. They have got certain manufacturers and men of influence to make a note of their name and address in their pocket-book. But nothing has come of it all. They were at first very hopeful. They thought each post would bring the expected letter. There was a woman in America who went every morning for ten years to the village postmaster to ask for a letter from her son, which he promised to send, but which had never come. But the embers have grown colder and colder still. Hope has flickered out. It is sad enough to be disappointed; but the sting of disappointment is when we are forgotten.

II. THREE BRIEF PIECES OF ADVICE TO THOSE IN SIMILAR CIRCUMSTANCES.

1. *Cease ye from man, whose breath is in his nostrils!* We cannot live without human sympathy and friendship. We long for the touch of the human hand and the sound of the human voice. We eagerly catch at any encouragement which some frail man holds out, as a drowning man catches at twigs floating by on the stream. But men fail us; even the best prove to be less able or less willing than we thought: the stream turns out to be a very turbid one when we reach it, in spite of all reports of its sufficiency. "Cursed be the man that trusteth in man, and maketh flesh his arm, and whose heart departeth from the Lord: for he shall be like the heath in the desert, and shall not see when good cometh; but shall inhabit the parched places in the wilderness, a salt land and not inhabited."

2. *Turn from the failure and forgetfulness of man to the constancy and faithfulness of God!* "He abideth faithful." He cannot promise and fail to perform. He says Himself: "Thou shalt not be forgotten by Me." A woman may forget her sucking child, and be unmindful of the son of her womb, "yet will I not forget thee." He may leave you long without succour. He may allow you to toil against a tempestuous sea until the fourth watch of the night. He may seem silent and austere, tarrying two days still in the same place, as if careless of the dying Lazarus. He may allow your prayers to accumulate like unopened letters on the table of an absent friend. But at last He will say, "O man, O woman, great is thy faith: be it unto thee even as thou wilt."

3. *Wait for God!* We are too feverish, too hasty, too impatient. It is a great mistake. Everything comes only to those

who can wait. "They that wait on the Lord shall inherit the
earth." You may have had what Joseph had when still a lad
—a vision of power and usefulness and blessedness. But you
cannot realize it in fact. All your plans miscarry. Every door
seems shut. The years are passing over you with the depressing
sense that you have not wrought any deliverance in the earth.
Now turn your heart to God; accept his will; tell Him that you
leave to Him the realization of your dream. "Wait on the
Lord, and keep his way, and He shall exalt thee to inherit the
land: when the wicked are cut off thou shalt see it." He may
keep you waiting a little longer; but you shall find Him verify
the words of one who knew by experience his trustworthiness:
"The salvation of the righteous is of the Lord; He is their
strength in the time of trouble. And the Lord shall help them,
and deliver them; He shall deliver them from the wicked and
save them, because they trust in Him."

III. THE LINKS IN THE CHAIN OF DIVINE PROVIDENCE.—
First, the wife of Potiphar makes a baseless charge, which leads
to Joseph's imprisonment; then, the young prisoner ingratiates
himself with the keeper of the prison, and is allowed to have
free access to the prisoners; then it happens at the very time
that two state officials are thrown into gaol on suspicion of
attempting to poison their royal master; then the verification
of Joseph's interpretation of their dreams shows that he is possessed of no common power; then that department of memory
in which Joseph's face and case are hidden becomes sealed,
lest anything premature should be attempted on his behalf;
then, after two full years, the king of Egypt dreams. To the
casual observer there might seem a great deal of chance in all
this; but the historian, directed by the Holy Spirit, lifts the
veil, and shows that God was working out, step by step, his
own infinite plans.

The dream was twice repeated, so similarly as to make it
evident to the dullest mind that something was intended of
unusual importance. The scene in each case was the river

bank; first the green margin of grass, next the rich alluvial soil. To say the least, it was a bad omen to see the lean kine devour the fat, and the withered ears devour the full: nor can we wonder that the monarch of a people who attached special importance to omens and portents should send in hot haste for the army of priests who were always in close attendance upon him; and who on this occasion were reinforced by all the wise men, adepts in this branch of science. But there was none that could interpret the dream of Pharaoh. "God made foolish the wisdom of this world."

Then, amid the panic of the palace, the butler suddenly remembered his prison experiences, and told the king of the young captive Hebrew. Pharaoh eagerly caught at the suggestion: he sent and called Joseph; and they brought him hastily out of the dungeon—the margin says, "they made him run." Still the king's impetuous speed was compelled to wait till he had shaved himself and changed his prison garb. Perfect cleanliness and propriety of dress were so important in the eyes of Egyptians that the most urgent matters were postponed until they were properly attended to. Alas, that men should be so careful of their appearance before one another, and so careless of their appearance before God! Many a man who would not think of entering a drawing-room if his linen were not snowy white is quite content to carry within his breast a heart as black as ink.

It is beautiful to notice Joseph's reverent references to God in his first interview with Pharaoh. "It is not in me: God shall give Pharaoh an answer of peace." "God hath showed Pharaoh what He is about to do." "The thing is established by God; and God will shortly bring it to pass." The hypocrite is quick enough to interlard his conversation with the name of God: no doubt this is owing to his belief that a true child of God will often do so; and there is some truth in the belief. When the heart is full of God, the tongue will be almost obliged to speak of Him; and all such references will be easy and natural as flowers in May. Oh that our inner life were more full of the power and love and presence of Jesus! If our hearts were inditing a good matter they would boil over, and we should speak more frequently of the things that touch our King. Joseph was not ashamed to speak of his God amid the throng of idolaters in the court of Egypt: let us not flinch from bearing our humble witness in the teeth of violent opposition and supercilious scorn.

This position of recognizing Jehovah being assumed and granted, there was no difficulty in interpreting the consumption of the seven good kine by the seven lean kine, and of the seven full ears by the seven empty ears, blasted by the east wind; or of indicating that the seven years of great plenty should be followed by seven years of famine, so sore that all the plenty should be forgotten in the land of Egypt, and that famine should consume the land.

Now that the interpretation is before us, it seems wonderful, not that Joseph gave it, but that the wise men of Pharaoh's court failed to discover it. But perhaps God ordered it that the diviners should be rendered stupid and "mad," so that an opportunity should be made for the advancement, to which, from his childhood, Joseph had been destined. In this, as so often befalls, there was an illustration of the Divine words, "Thou hast hid these things from the wise and prudent, and hast revealed them unto babes: even so, Father, for so it seemed good in thy sight."

Then, in the presence of the thronged and breathless court, surrounded by the evil eyes of the magicians, who could ill afford to surrender their prestige and place, or the rich emoluments of their office, the young Hebrew interpreted the royal dream. That dream was framed in a thoroughly Egyptian setting, and was connected with the Nile, whose waters were regarded by the natives with an enthusiastic regard, whether for their peculiarly luscious, refreshing, and nutritive qualities, or for the annual inundation which bore far afield the rich, fertilizing soil. Indeed, for these and similar considerations the river was the object of idolatrous worship. The buffalo, a species of ox, well-known anciently in Egypt, delights to stand in the water in hot countries, remaining for hours in that cooling bath, with all the body, except the head, immersed. The sight of horned cattle coming up out of a river would, therefore, not be a rare occurrence; and Joseph had no difficulty in carrying his audience with him, when he said that these seven kine—as also the seven ears of corn on one stalk, after the nature of that species of bearded wheat still known as Egyptian wheat—were emblems of seven years of great plenty throughout all the land of Egypt.

But perhaps the thing which gave Joseph most influence in that court was not his interpretation, but the wise and statesmanlike policy on which he insisted. As he detailed his successive recommendations: the appointment of a man discreet and wise with this exclusive business as his life-work; of the creation of a new department of public business for the purpose of gathering up the resources of Egypt in anticipation of the coming need; of the vast system of storage in the cities of the land—it was evident that he was speaking beneath the glow of a spirit not his own; and with a power which commanded the instant assent of the monarch and his chief advisers. "The thing was good in the eyes of Pharaoh, and in the eyes of all his servants. And Pharaoh said unto his servants, Can we find such an one as this is, a man in whom the Spirit of God is?" Oh that we might carry with us, even into business relationships, the evident stamp of the Spirit of God! It were worth languishing, even in a dungeon, if only we might have time to seek it. But it is to be had on easier terms: "Ask and have; seek and find; open your heart and receive."

There is an interesting illustration given to us here of the words, "Them that honour Me, I will honour." When Joseph had interpreted the dream and given his advice—little thinking as he did so that he was sketching his own future—Pharaoh said unto his servants, "Can we find such an one as this is, a man in whom is the Spirit of God?" Then he turned to Joseph and said, "Forasmuch as God hath showed thee this, there is none so discreet and wise as thou art: thou shalt be over my house, and according to thy word shall all my people be ruled: only in the throne will I be greater than thou. See, I have set thee over the whole land of Egypt."

It was a wonderful ascent, sheer in a single bound from the dungeon to the steps of the throne. His father had rebuked him; now Pharaoh, the greatest monarch of his time, welcomes him. His brethren despised him; now the proudest priesthood of the world opens its ranks to receive him by marriage into their midst, considering it wiser to conciliate a man who was from that moment to be the greatest force in Egyptian politics and life. The hands that were hard with the toils of a slave are adorned with a signet ring. The feet are no longer tormented by fetters; a chain of gold is linked around his neck. The coat of many colours torn from him by violence and defiled by blood, and the garment left in the hand of the adulteress, are exchanged for vestures of fine linen drawn from the royal wardrobe. He was once trampled upon as the offscouring of all things; now all Egypt is commanded to bow before him, as he rides forth in the second chariot, prime minister of Egypt, and second only to the king. What a comment is this on that rapturous outburst, on the model of which the Virgin Mother composed her happy ode!

> "The Lord killeth, and maketh alive;
>   He bringeth down to the grave,
>   And bringeth up.
> The Lord maketh poor, and maketh rich;
>   He bringeth low, and lifteth up.
> He raiseth up the poor out of the dust,
>   And lifteth up the beggar
>   From the dunghill,
> To set them among princes,
>   And to make them inherit
>   The throne of glory."

THE STEPS OF THE THRONE

All this happened because one day, for the sake of God, Joseph resisted a temptation to one act of sin. If he had yielded, we should probably never have heard of him again; he would have been slain by the siren who has slain so many more strong men, and would have gone down to the dark chambers of death. No happy marriage, no wife, no child, would have fallen to his lot. No honour or usefulness, or vision of the dear faces of his kin, would ever have enriched his life with their abundant blessing. What a good thing it was that he did not yield!

Let us stand firm; let us seek first the kingdom of God and his righteousness; let us deny ourselves immediate pleasure for the sake of the far-off harvest of content; let us honour God by obedience to his least command; let us dare to say, No; let us be willing to decrease. And then the tide will turn: God will not be unfaithful to forget; He will turn again and have mercy upon us, and will exalt us to inherit the earth.

And when that day comes, let us ascribe all to God. I admire the names which Joseph gave to his sons. They show the temper of his heart when in the zenith of his prosperity. Manasseh means "forgetting"—God had made him forget his toils. Ephraim means "fruitfulness"—God had caused him to be fruitful. Be true! *you* shall forget your sorrow and long waiting; *you* shall be fruitful. Then be sure and give God the praise.

IV. THE PARALLEL BETWEEN JOSEPH AND THE LORD JESUS. —It is surely more than a coincidence. "Coming events cast their shadows before." The Holy Spirit, enamoured with the mystery of love which was coming, anticipated its most striking features in the life of Joseph. Joseph was rejected by his brethren; Jesus by the Jews, his brethren according to the flesh. Joseph was sold for twenty pieces of silver to the Ishmaelites; Jesus was sold by the treachery of Judas for thirty pieces, and then handed over to the Gentiles. Joseph was cast into prison: Jesus abode in the grave. Joseph in prison was able to preach the gospel of deliverance to the butler; Jesus went and preached the gospel to the spirits in the prison. The two malefactors of the cross find their counterpart in Joseph's two fellow-prisoners. Joseph, though a Jew by birth and rejected by his own brethren, nevertheless was raised to supreme power in a Gentile state, and saved myriads of them from death; Jesus, of Jewish birth and yet disowned by Jews, has nevertheless been exalted to the supreme seat of power, and is now enthroned in the hearts of myriads of Gentiles, to whom He has brought salvation from death, and spiritual bread for their hunger. The very name that Pharaoh gave to Joseph meant "Saviour of the world"—our Saviour's title. Yes, and we must carry the parallel still farther. After Joseph had been for some time ruling and blessing Egypt, his very brethren came to him for forgiveness and help; so in days not far away we shall see the Jews retracing their steps and exclaiming—as thousands are now doing in Eastern Russia—"Jesus is our Brother." So all Israel shall be saved!

We have now, therefore, to think of Jesus as seated on his throne, Prime Minister of the universe, the Interpreter of his Father's will, the Organ and Executor of the Divine decrees. On his head are many crowns; on his finger is the ring of sovereignty; on his loins the girdle of power. Glistering robes of light envelop Him. And this is the cry which precedes Him, "Bow the knee!" Have *you* ever bowed the knee at his feet? It is of no avail to oppose Him. The tongue of malice and envy may traduce Him, and refuse to let Him reign. But nothing can upset the Father's decree and plan. "Yet have I set my Son upon my holy hill." "In his name every knee shall bow, and every tongue shall confess that He is Lord." Agree with Him quickly. Ground your arms at his feet. "Kiss the Son, lest He be angry."

V. THE WORLD'S NEED FOR CHRIST.—You remember Pharaoh's dream. Seven buffaloes, which had escaped from

THE STEPS OF THE THRONE

the torturing heat into the comparative coolness of the water, came up on to the banks and began feeding on the sedge. Shortly after, seven lean kine came up, and, finding nothing left for them to eat, by one of those strange transformations common to dreams, swallowed up their predecessors. So the seven shrivelled ears devoured those which were rank and good. This is a symbol of a fact that is always happening, and is happening now.

Our rulers, like Pharaoh, are having troublesome visions just now. In Europe and in England weak things are destroying the strong; hungry creatures are devouring the flourishing and the fat; the sterile is swallowing up the fruitful: and there is no visible improvement. Those who know how much we spend each year for drink and for our army; for extravagance and show—will understand what I mean. Oh, it is grievous to see how much is being squandered to no purpose on all these things, when our toiling masses are sinking deeper and deeper into misery and need! And where is the cure? It seems beyond our reach. Our wisdom, with its parliaments, its learned articles, its congresses, seems at its wits' end and non-plussed. At this very hour, for want of something better, millions of men are under arms to keep the hungry and weak from further devouring the flourishing and fat. For God Himself is bringing Egypt to despair, that it may learn the need of that Jesus who—like Joseph once—is now hidden from its view. Then these Bibles shall be searched for guidance, and places of Christian worship shall be crowded; and the Rejected One shall reign, and his bride shall be given Him. Then shall earth rejoice; for He cometh to rule in equity, and his reign is goodwill to men!

It may be that seven years of famine have been passing over you, devouring all that you had accumulated in happy bygone times, and leaving you bare. Do you not guess the reason? There is a rejected Saviour transferred to some obscure dungeon in your heart. There never can be prosperity or peace so long as He is there. Seek Him forthwith. Cause thyself to run to Him. Ask Him to forgive years of shameful neglect. Reinstate Him on the throne. Give the reins of power into his hand. And He shall restore to thee the years that the cankerworm has eaten.

VII

Joseph's First Interview with His Brethren
(Genesis XLII)

"Oh hateful spell of sin!—when friends are nigh
To make stern memory tell her tale unsought,
And raise accusing shades of hours gone by,
To come between us and all kindly thought!"
                                        KEBLE.

THE life of Joseph, as the Prime Minister of Egypt, was a very splendid one. Everything that could please the sense or minister to the taste was his. The walls of Egyptian palaces still exist in the rainless air to attest the magnificent provision that was made for all necessaries and luxuries. In point of fact, the civilization of our nineteenth century in many points has nothing of which to boast over that of the age in which he lived, and of which the record still remains. His palaces would consist of numberless rooms opening into spacious courts, where palms, sycamores, and acacia trees grew in rare luxuriance. The furniture, consisting of tables, couches, and consoles, would be elegantly carved from various woods, encrusted with ebony and adorned with gilding. Rare perfumes rose from vases of gold and bronze and alabaster; and the foot sank deep in carpets covering the floors, or trod upon the skins of lions and other ferocious beasts. Troops of slaves and officials ministered to every want. Choirs of musicians filled the air with sweet melody. Such is said to be a true description of the outward circumstances of Joseph's lot.

But though one of rare splendour, *his life must have been one of considerable anxiety*. He had to deal with a proud hereditary nobility, jealous of his power, and with a populace mad with hunger. During the first seven years of his premiership he went throughout all the land of Egypt superintending the dykes and ditches which should utilize as much as possible the unusual rise of the Nile; building vast granaries, and buying up a fifth of the vast profusion of grain. "The earth brought forth by handfuls; and Joseph gathered corn as the sand of the sea, very much, until he left numbering, for it was without number." All this must have involved a great deal of anxiety; it must have been difficult for this young foreigner to carry out his wide-reaching plans in face of the stolid apathy or the active opposition of great officials and vested interests.

He was, however, *eminently qualified for this work*; for there was something in him that could not be accounted for by any analysis of his brain. As Pharaoh had said most truly, "He was a man in whom was the Spirit of God." Oh, when will men learn that the Spirit of God may be in them when they are buying and selling, and arranging all the details of business or home? When will they believe that those will do their part best in the market-place, and in the house, who are most sensible of the gracious and forceful indwelling of the Holy Ghost? May God send us all the simple reverent spirit of this man, who amidst the splendour and business of his proud position set God always before his face! Such a temper of mind will make us a blessing to our times; for, at last, when the days of famine came, Joseph was able, as he afterwards said, to be a "father" unto Pharaoh, and to save the land.

All these events took time. Joseph was a lad of seventeen summers when he was torn away from his home; and he was a young man of thirty when he stood for the first time before Pharaoh. Seven years for the golden time of plenty must be added; and perhaps two more whilst the stores of the granaries were being slowly exhausted: so that probably twenty-five years had passed between the tragedy at the pit's mouth and the time of which we are thinking now. During those years the life in Jacob's camp had flowed uneventfully and quietly through the same unchanging scenes, like the course of some river in a flat, unbroken country, where a quick eye is required to discover the direction of the stream. The chief sign of the number of the slow passing years was the growing weakness in the old father's step and the increasing infirmity of his form. He pathetically speaks much of his "grey hairs". The sons of Israel had need to "carry Jacob their father". This was not simply the result of age, but of sorrow; he bore in his heart the scars of many wounds, the chief of which was grief for his beloved Joseph. It was grief that he was compelled very largely to nurse alone; and it was, perhaps, the keener because of the suspicions of foul play that seem to have suggested themselves to his mind. He went step by step down towards the grave "mourning for his son". He never could forget the sight of the blood-bedabbled coat, the dear relic of one whose face he never thought to see.

Meanwhile, the sons had become middle-aged men, with families of their own. They probably never mentioned that deed of violence to each other. *They did their best to banish the thought from their minds.* Sometimes in their dreams they may have caught a glimpse of that young face in its agony, or heard the beseechings of his anguished soul; but they sought to drown such painful memories by deep draughts of the Lethe-stream of forgetfulness. Conscience slept. Yet the time had come when God meant to use these men to found a nation. And in order to fit them for their high destiny it was necessary to bring them into a right condition of soul. Yet how could their soul be in health, so long as they had not repented of the sin which cast its lurid light over their history? The great Physician never heals over a wound from above, but from below, and after careful probing and searching. The foundations of noble character must touch the rock of genuine repentance. But it seemed almost impossible to secure repentance in those obtuse and darkened hearts. However, the Eternal brought it about by a number of wonderful providences; and as we study them, let us notice how God will subordinate all

the events of our outward lives to try us and prove us, and see
what there is in our hearts, and to bring us to Himself.

*This, then, is our theme: God's gracious methods of awaken-
ing the consciences of these men from their long and apparently
endless sleep.* And it is a theme well worth our study; for if
there is one thing more than another that is needed in Christian
congregations and in the world, it is the deep conviction of sin.
Well would it be if some resurrection trumpet could sound and
awaken the sleeping consciences of men, causing long-forgotten
but unforgiven sins to arise and come forth from their graves.
Of what use is it to present the Saviour to those who do not feel
to need Him? And who can scatter seed with hope of harvest,
unless the ploughshare has first driven its iron into the soil?

I. THE FIRST STEP TOWARDS THEIR CONVICTION WAS THE
PRESSURE OF WANT.—There was dearth in all lands; and the
famine reached even to the land of Canaan. Often before, in
the lives of the patriarchs, had they been driven by famine
down to Egypt; and Jacob aroused his sons from the hopeless
lethargy into which they were sinking by saying, "Why look
ye on one another? Behold, I have heard that there is corn
in Egypt; get you down there and buy for us, that we may
live and not die. And Joseph's ten brethren went down to
buy corn in Egypt."

So long as the hills were green and the pastures clothed
with flocks; so long as the valleys were covered over with corn
and rang with the songs of reapers—just so long Jacob might
have mourned alone; but Reuben, Simeon, and the rest of
them would have been unconcerned and content. But when
the mighty famine came, the hearts of these men were opened
to conviction; their carnal security was shattered; and they
were prepared for certain spiritual experiences of which they
would never have dreamed. Yes; and they were being prepared for the meeting with Joseph.

It is so that God deals with us. He breaks up our nest. He
loosens our roots. He sends a mighty famine which cuts away

the whole staff of bread. And at such times, weary, worn, and sad, we are prepared to confess our sins, and to receive the words of Christ, when He says, "Come unto Me, all ye that labour and are heavy-laden, and I will give you rest." Is your life just now passing through a time of famine? Do your supplies threaten to fail? Does your heart fail you, as you look forward to the disasters that menace you? Yet take courage; this is simply the motion of the current which is drifting you to Christ and to a better life. In after-days those men looked back upon that time of sore straitness as the best thing that could have happened to them: nothing less would have brought them to Joseph. Yes, and the time is coming when you will bless God for your times of sorrow and misfortune. You will say, "Before I was afflicted I went astray; but now have I kept thy Word."

II. THE SECOND STEP WAS THE ROUGH USAGE THEY RECEIVED AT THE HANDS OF JOSEPH.—It would seem that in some of the larger markets he superintended the sale of the corn himself. He may even have gone there on purpose, prompted by a sort of hope that he might catch sight of one of the Ishmaelites, whose faces he never could forget; or in some other way hear tidings of his home. He may have even cherished, and prayed over, the fancy that his brethren might come themselves. At last the looked-for day arrived. He was standing as usual at his post, surrounded by all the confusion and noise of an Eastern bazaar, when all of a sudden his attention was attracted by the entrance of those ten men. He looked with a fixed, eager look for a moment, his heart throbbing quickly all the while; and he needed no further assurance: "he knew them."

Evidently, however, they did not know him. How should they? He had grown from a lad of seventeen to a man of forty. He was clothed in pure white linen, with ornaments of gold to indicate his rank, a garb not altogether unlike that famous coat, which had wrought such havoc. He was governor of the land, and if they had thought of Joseph at all when entering that land (and no doubt they did), they expected to see him in the gangs of slaves manacled at work in the fields, or sweltering in the scorching brickyards, preparing material for the pyramids. So, in unconscious fulfilment of his own boyish dream, they bowed down themselves before him with their faces to the earth.

Joseph instantly saw that they failed to recognize him; and partly to ascertain if his brethren were repentant, partly in order to know why Benjamin was not with them, he made himself strange unto them. He spake roughly to them. He accused them of being spies. He refused to believe their statements, and put them in prison until they could be verified. He kept Simeon bound.

In all this, I believe *he repeated exactly the scene at the pit's mouth*; and indeed we may perhaps see what really happened there, reflected in the mirror of this scene. It is not unlikely that when they saw him coming towards them, in his prince-like dress, they had rushed at him, accusing him of having come to spy out their corrupt behaviour, and take back an evil report to their father, as he had done before: if so, this will explain why he now suddenly accused them of being spies. No doubt the lad protested that he was no spy—that he had only come to inquire after their welfare; but they had met his protestations with rude violence in much the same way as the rough-speaking governor now treated them. It may be that they had even thrust him into the pit with the threat to keep him there until his statements could be verified, in much the same way as Joseph now dealt with them; and Simeon may have been the ringleader. If this were the case—and it seems most credible—it is obvious that it was a powerful appeal to their conscience and memory, and one that could not fail to awaken both.

You remember the story of Hamlet. Hamlet's uncle murdered his brother, the father of Hamlet, and King of Denmark. The deed was done secretly; but the young prince knew of it, and instructed the players to repeat the murder, in dumb show, before the royal but guilty pair, and their guests. They did so. At last the king could bear it no more. He rose hastily from his seat and went from the hall, saying:

> *"Oh, my offence is rank, it smells to Heaven;*
> *It hath the primal eldest curse upon it,*
> *A brother's murder."*

And as those men, each in his dungeon, considered the usage which they had experienced, it must have vividly brought to their minds their treatment of that guileless lad, years on years before.

There is another story in the Old Testament of which we are reminded now—that scene at Zarephath when the child died, and the mother burst into the presence of the prophet saying, "Hast thou come to call my sin to remembrance?" She had tried to forget her sin. She had buried it deep in a far down dungeon, like that in the old castle of Chillon beneath the blue waters of Geneva's lake. But there was something in that dead child which brought it all back to her mind; she lived it over again: but not its pleasure, that had long since passed away; only its pain was left.

Memory is one of the most wonderful processes of our nature. It is the faculty that enables us to record and recall the past. If it were not for this power the mind would remain for ever in the blank condition of childhood, and all that had ever passed before it would leave no more impression than images do upon the plain surface of a reflecting mirror. But important as it is, it conducts its operations in perfect mystery. The room is shuttered from all human gaze; the camera is covered by a black veil. This, however, is the one fact of interest to us— that it has a universal retentiveness. Nothing has ever passed athwart it that has not left a record on its plastic slabs.

It is important, however, to distinguish between memory and recollection. We remember all things: there is a record of everything that ever we saw or did, somewhere in the archives of memory; but we cannot always recollect an incident, or recall it at the required moment. Supposing you were never to burn your letters, but kept them all in one huge box—that would resemble memory; but supposing you were never to index or classify them, so as to be unable readily to lay your hands on the one required—that would be like a failure of recollection; whilst a ready recollection would find its analogy in the ease with which you could produce a required letter at a given time. The failure to find a letter would not argue that the letter was not in the box, but simply that the classification was bad; so the failure to recall the past does not argue that it is lost to memory, but simply that the power of recollection is feeble. In other words, our memory really retains everything; and though sometimes our recollection is bad, yet a very trivial thing may excite it and enable it to fetch up things long past from the deep compartments of memory into which they have been cast, and in which they have been unceasingly held.

The reader may have been brought up in a house surrounded by an old-fashioned country garden; but you have not thought of it for years, till the other day you happened to see a plant or smell a scent peculiarly associated with it, which brought the whole back to your recollection. So is it with sin. Long years ago, you may have committed some sin; you have tried to forget it. It has not been forgiven and put away; you have almost succeeded in dropping it from your thoughts: but believe me, it is still there; and the most trivial incident may at any moment bring it all back upon your conscience, as vividly as if committed only yesterday. If sin is forgiven, it is indeed forgotten: God says, "I will remember it no more." But if only forgotten, and not forgiven, it may have a most unexpected and terrible awakening.

This was the case with Joseph's brethren. They said one to another, as they heard the reiterated demand of the strange governor for evidence that they were not spies, "We are verily guilty concerning our brother; in that we saw the anguish of his soul, when he besought us, and we would not hear: therefore is this distress come upon us."

III. The Third Step towards Conviction was the giving of Time for them to listen to God's Spirit, speaking to them in the Silence of the Prison-cell.—Without the work of the Holy Ghost they might have felt remorse, but not guilt. It is not enough to feel that sin is a blunder and a mistake, but not guilt. This sense of sin, however, is the prerogative of the Spirit of God. He alone can convict of sin. When He is at work, the soul cries out, "Woe is me, I am a sinful man!" "We are verily *guilty* concerning our brother."

Will not these words befit some lips that read these pages? Are *you* not verily guilty? In early life you may have wronged some man or some woman. You may have taught some young lad to swear. You may have laughed away the early impressions from some anxious seeker, until they fled to return no more. You may not have done your best to save those committed to your care. And now others seem to be treating you as you treated the associates of earlier days. You now are eager for salvation; and you learn the bitterness of being ridiculed, thwarted, tempted, and opposed. You recall the past; it flashes before you with terrible intensity. You cry, "God forgive me! I am verily guilty concerning that soul whom I betrayed or wronged." And this is the work of the Holy Spirit. Let Him have his blessed way with you till you are led by Him to the foot of that tree which buds like Aaron's rod, though for eighteen hundred years it has ceased to grow, and the leaves of which are for the nations!

There is at least one Brother whom you have wronged. Need I mention his name? He is not ashamed to call you brother; but you have been ashamed of Him. He did not withhold Himself from the cross; but you have never thanked Him. He has never ceased to knock at the door of your heart for admittance to bless you; but you have kept Him waiting amid the dropping dews of night. He has freely offered you the greatest gifts; but you have trampled them beneath your feet, and done despite to Him, and crucified Him afresh. There is, no doubt, a time coming when the Jews shall say of Him, whom they once rejected and put into the pit of death, but who has since been giving corn to the Gentiles, "We are verily guilty concerning our Brother." But these words may also be humbly and sorrowfully appropriated by many of us. We must plead, "Guilty! guilty! guilty! guilty concerning our Brother!"

Whilst these men spoke thus, Joseph stood by them. There was no emotion on those compressed features, no response in those quiet eyes. "They wist not that he understood them." Ah, how often do anguished souls go to priests, ministers, and friends, with the bitter tale of anguish! They wist not that One is standing by who hears and understands all, and longs to throw aside every barrier in order to bring them aid. True, He speaks to them by an interpreter; but if they would only speak straight to Him, He would speak directly to their waiting hearts.

There is a curious contrast in the twenty-fourth verse. First, we learn that "he turned himself about from them and wept"; and next we are told that he "took Simeon and bound him before their eyes". The brethren saw only the latter of these two actions, and must have thought him rough and unkind. How they must have trembled in his presence! But they knew not the heart of tender love that was beating beneath all this seeming hardness. Nor could they guess that the retention of Simeon was intended to act as a silken cord to bring the brothers back to him, and as part of the process of awakening the memory of another brother, whom they had lost years before.

It is thus continually in life's discipline. We suffer, and suffer keenly. Imprisoned, bereaved, rebuked, we count God harsh and hard. We little realize how much pain He is suffering as He causes us pain; or how the tender heart of our Brother is filled with grief, welling up within Him as He makes Himself strange, and deals so roughly with us. If we could but see the tender face behind the vizor, and know how noble a heart beats beneath the mailed armour, we should feel that we were as safe amid his rebukes as ever we were amid his tenderest caresses.

There were alleviations also in their hardships. The sacks were filled with corn; provision was given for the journey home, so that they needed not to come on the stores they were carrying back for their households; and every man's money was returned in his sack's mouth (verse 25). All this was meant in tender love; but their hearts failed them with fear, as they emptied their sacks and saw the bundles of money fall out among the corn. A guilty conscience misinterprets the kindest gifts and mercies which God sends to us, and with evil ingenuity distils poison out of the sweetest flowers. How often, like these men, we cry, "What hath God done to us?" and are filled with fear, when, in point of fact, God's dealings with us brim with blessing, and are working out a purpose of mercy which shall make us rejoice all our days.

There is no lot, however hard, without its compensations. Be sure to look out for these. Prize the little touches of tender love which reveal the heart of Jesus, as a girl will dwell upon the slightest symptoms of an affection which, for some reason, must be concealed beneath a strange and unconcerned exterior. Amidst his chastenings, the Master inserts some delicate souvenirs of his love to keep the heart from entire despair. Make much of them until the discipline is over, and the sun of his regard bursts from all restraining clouds.

> *"Judge not the Lord by feeble sense,*
> *But trust Him for His grace;*
> *Beneath a frowning Providence*
> *He hides a smiling face."*

VIII

Joseph's Second Interview with His Brethren
(Genesis XLIII)

"Kind hearts are here; yet would the tenderest one
Have limits to its mercy: God has none.
And man's forgiveness may be true and sweet,
But yet he stoops to give it. More complete
Is Love that lays forgiveness at thy feet,
And pleads with thee to raise it. Only heaven
Means crowned, not vanquished, when it says 'Forgiven!'"
A. A. Procter.

WHERE is there such another story as this of Joseph? It seems sometimes impossible to believe that the events happened thirty-five centuries ago, in the solemn, rainless land of the Nile and the Pyramids. They might have occurred within our own memory, the experience is so natural, so life-like, so like our own. And yet orientalists assure us that, in its minutest details, it is verified by the paintings which, to this day, exist on the walls of palaces and temples, unimpaired and fresh.

I feel it impossible to dwell on it line by line; I must content myself with taking only the broad outlines of the story.

Our next chapter will deal with that affecting scene, when Joseph caused every man to go out from him, while he cast aside his dignity, stepped down from his throne, and fell upon the necks of his brethren and wept. We have a lesser task just now, yet full of interest; we have to consider the successive steps by which that wayward family was brought into a position in which its members could be forgiven and blessed. May the Holy Spirit help us to understand this; because Joseph, who was exalted from the pit to the palace, is an evident picture of Him who lay in the grave, but is now exalted to the right hand of the Father to give repentance unto Israel and the remission of sins! And as we review the successive steps by which Joseph led his brethren, we shall probably catch a glimpse of those various processes by which the Saviour humbles us and leads us to Himself. Should these words be read by the members of some family which is living in this famine-stricken world, minding only the things of sense and sin, ignorant of the great Brother who lives yonder on the throne of God and loves us—let them read, mark, learn, and inwardly digest them, for they may shed a light on some dark landings of their life, and explain things hard as the riddle of the Sphinx.

I. THERE WAS THE PRESSURE OF POVERTY AND SORROW (xliii. 1). Jacob had never turned his thoughts to Egypt if there had been plenty in Canaan. The famine drove the sons of Israel into Egypt to buy corn. And even though poor Simeon was bound in Egypt, the brothers had not gone a second time if it had not been for the rigour of that necessity, which sometimes drives the most timid birds and deer to the homes and haunts of men. At first the old father strongly opposed the thought of their taking Benjamin, even if they went themselves; and his children lingered.

There is a touching picture given of the conversation between the old man and his sons, a kind of council of war. Reuben seems already to have lost the priority which his birthright would have secured, and Judah held the place of spokesman and leader amongst the brethren. He undertook to deal with the old man for the rest. At the outset, Jacob's request that they should go down to buy food was met with the most distinct refusal, unless Benjamin was permitted to accompany them. And when he complained of their having betrayed the existence of another brother, the whole of them vindicated their action, and declared that they could not have done otherwise. At last Judah made himself personally responsible for the lad's safety, a pledge which, as we shall see, he nobly redeemed. And so, at last, the old man yielded, proposing only that they should take a present to mollify the ruler's heart, a double money to replace what had been returned in their sacks, and uttering a fervent prayer to the Almighty on their behalf. Thus God in his mercy shut up every other door but the one through which they might find their way to plenty and blessedness. There was no alternative but to go down to Egypt.

So is your life. You have had all that this world could give. Beauty, money, youth, health, success, have come up and poured their horns of plenty into your lap. You have had all that man could wish. But what has been your state of heart meanwhile? Have you bethought yourself of your ill-treatment of your great Elder Brother? Have you set your affections upon things above? Have you lived for that world which lies beyond the narrow horizon of the visible? You know you have not. So God has called for a famine on your land, and broken the whole staff of your bread. You have lost situation and friends. Your business is broken. Beauty, youth, health—all have vanished. Joseph is not; Simeon is not; and Benjamin is on the point of being taken away. Everything has been against you.

It is a severe measure: how will you bear it? In the first burst of the tempest, you say stubbornly, "I will not go down; I will not yield; I will stand out to the last." But, beware! It is a fatal mistake to wrestle against the love of God. Jacob tried it by the Jabbok ford; and he limped on a halting thigh until he gathered his feet up into his deathbed. God will have his way at last if not at first. The famine must continue until the wanderer arises to return to the Father, with words of penitent contrition on his lips. It is in vain to row to bring the ship to land: the sea will not cease her raging until the runaway prophet is on his way back to his home. "I will be," saith the Lord, "unto Ephraim as a lion, and as a young lion to the house of Judah. I, even I, will tear and go away; and none shall rescue. I will go and return to my place, till they

acknowledge their offence, and seek my face; in their affliction they will seek Me early." Oh that your reply might
be!—"Come, and let us return unto the Lord; for He hath
torn, and He will heal us; He hath smitten, and He will bind
us up."

II. THERE WAS THE AWAKENING OF CONSCIENCE. For twenty
years conscience had slept. And as long as this was the case
there could be no real peace between Joseph and his brethren.
They could never feel sure that he had forgiven them. *He*
would always feel that there was a padlock on the treasure-
store of his love. You never can feel at perfect rest with your
friend, so long as there is some unexplained wrong between
you. Conscience must awake and slowly tread the aisles of
the temple of penitence, telling the beads of confession. This
is the clue to the understanding of Joseph's behaviour.

*Joseph, to arouse their dormant consciences, repeated as
nearly as possible to them, their treatment of himself.* This
has already engaged our thought. "Ye are spies," was the
echo of their own rough words to himself. The prison, in
which they lay for three days, was the counterpart of the pit in
which they placed *him*. Men will best learn what is the true
nature of their own iniquities when they experience the treatment which they meted out to others. And Joseph's device
was a success. Listen to their moan, "We are verily guilty
because of our brother."

Here again is a clue to the mysteries of our own lives. God
sometimes allows us to be treated as we have treated Him,
that we may see our offence in its true character, and may be
obliged to turn to Him with words of genuine contrition. Your
child has turned out badly enough: you did everything for
him; now he refuses to do what you wish, and even taunts
you. Do you feel it? Perhaps this will reveal to you what
God feels, in that, though He has nourished and brought you
up, yet you have rebelled against Him. Your neighbour, when
in trouble, came to you for help, and promised to repay you

with interest, with many protestations: now he prospers, and you ask him to repay you; but he either laughs at you, or tells you to wait. Do you feel it? Ah, now you know how God feels, He who helped you in distress, to whom you made many vows, but who reminds you in vain of all the past. You know what it is to stand day after day a suppliant, waiting at a gate which never opens, listening for a footstep that never comes. Do you feel it? Ah, now you know what *He* feels who twenty years ago stood at the door of your heart and knocked, and is there now waiting, full-handed, to enrich you. That conscience must indeed be fast in slumber that awakens not at such appeals.

III. THERE WAS THE DISPLAY OF MUCH TENDER LOVE TOWARDS THEM. As soon as Joseph espied them he invited them to his own table to feast with him. The brothers were brought into his house, where every kindness was shown to them; as if, instead of being poor shepherds, they were the magnates of the land. Their fears as to the return of the money were allayed by the pious, though prevaricating, assurance of the steward that if they had discovered it in their sacks it must have been put there by God, as there was no doubt about the price of their corn having come into his hands. And when Joseph came they prostrated themselves before him in striking fulfilment of his own boyish dream. He asked them tenderly about the well-being of their father; and there must have been a pathos in his words to Benjamin which would have revealed the whole secret if they had not been so utterly unprepared to find Joseph beneath the strange guise of the great Egyptian governor.

What an inimitable touch is that, which tells us how Joseph's heart welled up into his eyes, so that he needed to make haste to conceal the bursting emotions, which threatened to overmaster him. "He sought where to weep, and he entered into his chamber, and wept there. And he washed his face, and went out, and refrained himself; and said, Set on bread."

There may be prophetic touches here. And we may yet see the counterpart of this scene literally fulfilled, when the Lord comes forward to recognize and receive his ancient people. *But in the meanwhile what shall we say of his love to ourselves?* Ah, we need the fervid heart and the burning words of a Rutherford to deal with such a theme. The rejected Brother may seem strange and rough. He may cause sorrow. He may bind Simeon before our eyes. But, beneath all, He loves us with a love in which is concentrated the love of all parents to their children, and of all friends for their beloved. And that love is constantly devising means of expressing itself. It puts money into our sacks; it invites us to its home, and spreads banquets before us; it inclines stewards to meet us peacefully; it washes our feet; it takes a tender interest in those we love; it wishes us grace from God; it adjusts itself to our temperaments and puts us at our ease, so that gleams of light as to the love of Jesus strike into our hearts! He feels yearnings over us which He restrains, and dares not betray till the work of conviction is complete, and He can pour the full tides of affection on us, without injury to others or harm to ourselves.

IV. THERE WAS THE DESTRUCTION OF THEIR SELF-CONFIDENCE. They thought their *word* was good; but when they told their family history, Joseph refused to believe it, and said it must be proved. They were confident in their *money*; and as they paid down the shining pieces, they congratulated themselves that in this respect at least they were even with this rough governor—now at least he cannot touch them or count them as defaulters. But when they reached their first halting-place on their way home, "as one of them opened his sack to give his ass provender, he espied his money; for, behold, it was in the sack's mouth: and he said unto his brethren, My money is restored; and lo, it is even in my sack: and their heart failed them, and they were afraid, saying one to another, What is this that God hath done unto us?"

How often this happens in the experience of sinful men!
They want to stand right with God; but they like to do so in
their own way. Like Cain, they bring the fruit which their own
hands have raised. Like these men, they bring their hard-earned
money. Like the Pharisees, they bring prayers and tithes and
gifts. But when these gifts have been laid upon the altar, their
donors are amazed to find that they count for nothing, *and are
even given back.* No! the mercy of God, which is the true
bread of the spirit, is not to be bought by anything we can
bring; it must be received as a gift without money and without
price. Jacob said, "Peradventure it was an oversight": but it
was not; it was part of a deeply-laid plan, designed and executed
for a special purpose. There is no oversight, and no peradventure, in the life of man.

> *"All nature is but art unknown to thee;*
> *All chance, direction which thou canst not see;*
> *All discord, harmony not understood;*
> *All partial evil, universal good."*

They were confident also in their *integrity.* Little knowing
what was in the sack of one of them, when the morning was
light they started on their return journey for the second time.
They were in high spirits. Simeon was with them; so was
Benjamin, notwithstanding the nervous forebodings of the old
father. They were evidently in high favour with the governor,
else they had not been treated to so grand a feast on the
previous day. Their sacks were as full as they could possibly
hold. But they had hardly got clear of the city gate, when
they were arrested by the steward's voice. "Stop! Stop! Why
have ye rewarded evil for good?" And they said, "Wherefore
saith my lord these words? Behold, the money which we found
in our sacks' mouths we brought again unto thee: how then
should we steal silver or gold out of thy lord's house?" And,
so sure were they of their integrity, that they went further and
said: "With whomsoever thy master's cup is found, let him

die, and we also will be my lord's bondmen." "Then they speedily took down every man his sack to the ground, and opened every man his sack." And the steward searched them there on the bare road, beginning with the eldest to the youngest, "*and the cup was found in Benjamin's sack.*" Well might Judah and his brethren come to Joseph's house and fall before him on the ground, and say, "What shall we say unto my lord? What shall we speak? or how shall we clear ourselves? God hath found out the iniquity of thy servants." They were stripped of every rag of self-confidence, and were shut up to his uncovenanted mercy.

Some men resemble Benjamin. They are naturally guileless and beautiful. Some faint traces of original innocence linger about them. Their type is shown forth in the young man whom Jesus loved, as he stood before Him breathless with haste, protesting that he had kept all the commandments blameless from his youth. We do not reckon sin to such; and they do not reckon it to themselves. The publican and the sinner may stand in urgent need of the blood of Christ; but surely nitre and soap will suffice for them. But this reasoning is full of flaws. Such people seem good, only because they are compared with sinners of a blacker dye. Compare them with the only standard of infinite purity; and they are infinitely condemned. "If I wash myself with snow-water, and make my hands never so clean, yet shalt Thou plunge me in the ditch, and mine own clothes shall abhor me." The servants think the linen clean as it hangs upon the line, contrasted with the dingy buildings around; but when the snowflakes fall, they wonder that they never before discerned its lack of whiteness. The schoolboy thinks his writing good, only so long as he contrasts it with that of a worse penman than himself; but he soon alters his opinion when he catches sight of the copy. So estimable characters pride themselves on their morality, only until they behold the seamless robes of Christ, whiter than any fuller on earth could whiten them. But *these* must be taught their utter sinfulness; *they* must learn their secret unworthiness; *they* must be made to take their stand with the rest of men. Benjamin must be reduced to the level of Simeon and Judah. The cup must be found in *Benjamin's* sack.

A preacher of the Gospel was once speaking to an old Scotchwoman, who was commonly regarded as one of the most devout and respectable people in that part of the country. He was impressing on her her need of Christ. At last, with tears in her eyes, she said, "Oh, sir, I have never missed a Sabbath at the kirk; and I have read my Bible every day; and I have prayed and done good deeds to my neighbours; and I have done all I knew I ought to do: and now do you mean to tell me that it must all go for nothing?" He answered, "Well, you have to choose between trusting in these and trusting in the redemption which God offers you in Christ. You cannot have both. If you are content to part company with your own righteousness, the Lord will give you his; but if you cling to your Bible-reading and Sabbath-keeping and good deeds, the Lord's righteousness cannot be yours." It was quite a spectacle, he said afterwards, to see that old woman's face. *The cup was found in Benjamin's sack.* For some time she sat in silence, her elbows on the table, her face buried in her hands: a great struggle was going on within. At length the tears began to stream from her eyes, and, lifting up her clasped hands to heaven, she cried out, "Oh, my God, they shall all gang for naething!" In a moment more she cast herself on her knees and accepted the Lord Jesus as her Saviour. It is when the cup is found in Benjamin's sack that he, too, is brought to the feet of Jesus.

There is a stolen cup in your sack, my respectable, reputable, moral friend. You are probably unconscious of it. You pride yourself upon your blameless life. You suppose that Christ Himself has no controversy with you. But if you only knew, you would see that you are robbing Him of his own. You use for yourself time and money and talents which He bought with his own precious blood, and which He meant to be a chosen vessel unto Himself. It is remarkable that you, who are so scrupulous in paying every man his dues, should be so careless of the daily treachery of which you are guilty in defrauding the Lord of his own purchase. But if you hide the unwelcome truth from yourself, you cannot hide it from your Lord. "Wot ye not that such an one as He can certainly divine?" "He searcheth the hearts and trieth the reins of the children of men." And "he that is first in his own cause seemeth just; but his neighbour cometh and searcheth him."

How then shall we act? First, *Do not linger.* "Except we had lingered, surely now ere this we should have returned twice." Except you had lingered, ere this you would have become an earnest, happy Christian. "The angels hastened Lot as he lingered." Make haste! The door is shutting; and when it shuts it will lock itself. The entrance is nearly bricked up. The hour-glass is nearly run out, and when its last grain has gone the court of mercy will close.

Secondly, *Make full confession or restitution.* "They came near to the steward of Joseph's house and communed with him," and told him all about the finding of the money, and offered it back in full weight. Commune with Christ as you close this story. Tell Him all that is in your heart. Restore what you have taken wrongfully from Him or from others. Make full and thorough restitution. "When I kept silence, my bones waxed old through my roaring all the day long; for day and night thy hand was heavy upon me: my moisture was turned into the drought of summer. I acknowledged my sin unto Thee, and mine iniquity have I not hid. And thou forgavest the iniquity of my sin." "He that covereth his sins shall not prosper; but whoso confesseth and forsaketh them shall have mercy."

Thirdly, *Throw yourself on the mercy of Christ.* Judah did not excuse himself or his brethren; he had been non-suited if he had. He adopted a wiser course—he pleaded for mercy. Mercy for their own sakes! mercy for the lad's sake! mercy for the sake of the old father with his grey hairs at home! Try that plea with your Lord. You will find that it will not fail you. Say, as you beat upon your breast, "Be merciful unto me, *the* sinner!" He will not be able to refrain. He will say, in broken accents, "Come near unto Me; I am Jesus your Brother: your sins nailed Me to the cross, but speak of it no more; grieve not for it. God has overruled it for good, that I might save your lives by a great deliverance."

IX

JOSEPH MAKING HIMSELF KNOWN
(GENESIS XLV)

"Thou know'st our bitterness—our joys are Thine—
No stranger Thou to all our wanderings wild:
Nor could we bear to think, how every line
Of us, thy darkened likeness, and defiled,
Stands in full sunshine of thy piercing eye,
But that Thou call'st us Brethren: sweet repose
Is in that word—the Lord who dwells on high
Knows all, yet loves us better than He knows."
KEBLE.

"THE cup was found in Benjamin's sack." What a discovery
was that! There in the open road, in the early morning light,
as the villagers were passing into the city with melons and
leeks and onions, and as the city was beginning to bestir itself,
the cup of the great Premier, in whose hands was the power
of life and death, was found lying in the corn, half hidden, as
by stealth. But how did it come there? The brothers could
not tell. They neither could nor would believe that Benjamin
had known anything of it. Yet how to explain the mystery
was a problem they could not solve. It seemed as if some
evil genius were making them its sport, first in putting the
money in their sacks, and then in concealing the cup there.

And yet, in a moment, each brother must have wished that
the cup could have been found in any sack rather than in
Benjamin's. They all remembered their father's strange un-
willingness to let him come. The old man had seemed to have
a presentiment of coming disaster. When first they returned
from Egypt he said decisively, "My son shall not go down

with you; for his brother is dead, and he is left alone: if mischief befall him by the way in the which ye go, then shall ye bring down my grey hairs with sorrow to the grave." And when the pressure of famine compelled them, the last words of the timid and stricken parent were, "God Almighty give you mercy before the man, that he may send away your other brother, and Benjamin. If I be bereaved of my children, I am bereaved." All the time his heart was filled with the presages of coming sorrow; and now those forebodings seemed about to be fulfilled. Each of those men must have thought to himself, as he followed in the sad procession back, "How dare I face my father? When first we reach home, he will be sure to look first for Benjamin; and if he does not see him with us, he will receive a stab of grief in his heart from which he will never rally, and his grey hairs will go down with sorrow to the grave." But there was nothing for it except to reload their asses and return. Oh, how different the road seemed to what it had been a little before! The same sun was shining; the same busy scene surrounded them—but a dark veil was spread over sky and earth.

Let us study the scene that followed. It demands our care; for it throws light on our Lord's dealings with contrite souls, and it is an anticipation of the time when Israel shall seek with tears unto Him who once was nailed by them to the cross, but who is "exalted a Prince and a Saviour, to give repentance unto Israel, and forgiveness of sins."

I. NOTICE THE CIRCUMSTANCES IN WHICH THEY FOUND THEM-SELVES. *Their conscience was now awakened, and it was ill at ease.* There was no need for them to mention that crime of twenty years before; and yet it seemed impossible for them to refrain from mentioning that which was uppermost in their minds. They were evidently thinking deeply of that dark deed by the pit's mouth; their own sorrows had brought the sorrows of that frail young lad to their minds; they could not but feel

JOSEPH MAKING HIMSELF KNOWN 91

that there was some connection between the two; and thus the first words uttered by Judah their spokesman, as they entered the audience-chamber of Joseph, betrayed the dark forebodings of their thoughts: "What shall we say unto my Lord? What shall we speak? or how shall we clear ourselves? God hath found out the iniquity of thy servants."

God will always find out our iniquity. The sleuth-hound is on your track: it may take years to run you down; but it will never leave the trail until it has discovered your hiding-place and found you out. "Be sure your sin will find you out." Tens of years may pass over your life; and like these brethren you may be congratulating yourself that the sin is forgotten, and you are safe: and then a train of circumstances, little suspected, but manipulated by a Divine hand, will suddenly bring the truth to light, and write God's sentence in flaming characters upon the walls of the house in which you riot in careless ease. The unforgiven sinner is never safe. A terrible incident in point is recorded by Dr. Donne, once Prebendary of St. Paul's. On one occasion some excavations were being made in the precincts of the cathedral, and amongst other relics thrown up to the surface, there was a skull with a nail in it. He happened to be standing by; and having taken up the skull, and examined it, he asked the old sexton if he knew whose it was, and how the owner died. "Ah," said he, carelessly, "it is the skull of an aged man, who died very suddenly some years ago: his wife is living yet; she married again soon after his death." Dr. Donne found her out, and confronted her with the skull. The woman turned at once deadly pale; and confessed that she had taken her husband's life, and that she had no rest since by day or by night. This is a terrible example of a frequent law of God's world. And if all sin is not traced home to its authors in *this* world, at least there is enough to show how terrible that moment will be, when, at the "great white throne," the secrets of all hearts will be disclosed, and God will bring to light the hidden things of darkness. There is absolutely no chance of escape for a man, save in the wounds of Jesus; these are the city of refuge into which the pursuer cannot enter, and in which the fugitive is safe.

But, in addition, they felt that they were absolutely in Joseph's power. There he stood, second to none but Pharaoh in all the land of Egypt. Legions of warriors, like those depicted on the pyramids, were at his beck and call. If he had said that these men were all to be taken and imprisoned for life, or that Benjamin should be retained whilst the others were set free, there was absolutely no appeal: none could hinder him for a single moment. And the counterpart of this must surely be an alarming thought to the awakened sinner—that he is entirely at the mercy of the Judge of the quick and dead. There is none that can deliver out of his hand, or say, "What doest Thou?" The lamb in the power of the lion, the moth in the grasp of the hand, are not more entirely helpless than are sinners in the hand of God. "Agree with thine adversary quickly, whilst thou art in the way with him; lest haply the adversary deliver thee to the judge, and the judge deliver thee to the officer, and thou be cast into prison."

Moreover, they saw that appearances were strongly against them. There was no doubt that the cup had been found in Benjamin's sack; and though they were certainly innocent of the theft, yet they could not but feel that they were unable to clear or excuse themselves. As far as the evidence went, it pointed clearly and decisively to their guilt.

The divining cup is familiar enough to all students of ancient literature. It was sometimes made of crystal and of precious stones; and it was supposed that all secrets would be reflected by the liquid it contained. Homer sings of the cup of Nestor. And our own Spenser tells us how the royal maiden, Britomart, found Merlin's cup in her father's closet, and used it to discover a secret which closely concerned her. We, of course, do not believe that Joseph used such a cup for such a purpose; but it was his desire to maintain the character of an Egyptian of high rank. All Egyptian noblemen used such a cup. To appeal to it was most natural; and in their conscience-stricken condition, the brothers were too depressed to contest its decisions, or to ask for one more decisive test of their innocence or guilt.

II. NOTICE THEIR BEHAVIOUR. "*They fell before him on the ground.*" As they did so, they unconsciously fulfilled his own prediction, uttered when a boy. How vividly that memorable dream of the harvest field must have occurred to Joseph's mind! Here were their sheaves making obeisance to his sheaf, standing erect in the midst.

But who was to be their spokesman? Reuben had always had something to say in self-justification, and had been so sure that all would be right that he had pledged the lives of his children to his father for the safety of Benjamin; but *he* is dumb. Simeon was probably the cruel one, the instigator of the crime against Joseph; but *he* dares not utter a word. Benjamin, the blameless one, the prototype of the young man whom Jesus loved, is convicted of sin, and has nought to say. Who then is to speak? There is only one, Judah, who at the pit's mouth had diverted the brothers from their first thought of murder. And notice how he speaks. He does not attempt to hold up any extenuating circumstances, or to explain the past, or to excuse Benjamin or themselves. He throws himself helplessly on Joseph's mercy: "What shall we say unto my lord? what shall we speak? or how shall we clear ourselves?"

This is a good example for us to follow still. There is no doubt about our guilt. We are verily guilty concerning our treatment of that great Brother-man, who once lay in the pit, but who is now seated at the right hand of power. If we try to extenuate our faults, to excuse ourselves, to explain away the past, we shall only make bad worse: we shall be brought face to face with the damning evidence of our guilt; every mouth will be stopped; and we shall be obliged to cry, "God hath found out the iniquity of his servants." But if we throw ourselves on his mercy, we cannot fail.

We stand on surer ground than ever they did. They had no
idea of the gentleness of Joseph's heart; they had not seen him
turn aside to weep; they had not understood why on one occasion he had hastened from their presence; they could not guess
how near the surface lay the fountains of his tears. They only
knew him as rough, and stern, and hard. "The man, who is
lord of the land, spake roughly to us." But we know the
gentleness of the Lord Jesus. We have seen his tears over
Jerusalem; we have listened to his tender invitations to come
to Him; we have stood beneath his cross and heard his last
prayers for his murderers, and his words of invitation to the
dying thief; we know that He will not break the bruised reed,
nor quench the smoking flax. We then need not fear for the
issue when we cast ourselves upon his mercy. We then need not
stand trembling in the ante-chamber, saying, "If I perish, I
perish." We need not look nervously towards his throne to
see if the golden sceptre of his grace is extended towards us.
Failure and rejection are alike impossible to the soul that pleads
guilty, and that casts itself on the mercy of God which is in
Jesus Christ our Lord.

*In all literature, there is nothing more pathetic than this
appeal of Judah.* The eagerness that made him draw near;
the humility that confessed Joseph's anger might righteously
burn, since he was as Pharaoh; the picture of the old man,
their father, bereft of one son, and clinging to this little one,
the only relict of his mother; the recital of the strain which
the governor had imposed on them, by demanding that they
should bring their youngest brother down; the story of their
father's dread, only overmastered by the imperious demand of
a hunger that knew no law, and brooked no check; the vivid
picture of the father's eagerness again to see the lad, in whose
life his own was bound up; the heart-breaking grief at not
seeing him amongst them; the heroic offer to stay there a
slave, as Benjamin's substitute, if only the lad might go home;
the preference of a life of slavery rather than to behold the
old man sinking with sorrow into his grave—all this is touched

with master-hand. Oh, how much of poetry and pathos lie behind some of the roughest men, only waiting for some great sorrow to smite open the upper crust, and bore the Artesian well! But if a rough man could plead like this, think, ah think, what must not those pleadings be which Jesus offers before the throne! What moonbeams are to sunshine; what the affection of a dog is to the passionate love of a noble man —such is the pleading of Judah compared to the intercession of our great High-Priest! We have an Advocate in the Court of King's Bench who never lost a case: let us put ourselves into his hands, and trust Him when He says, "I have prayed for thee." "Such a High-Priest became us."

Thus Joseph's object was attained. He had wished to restore them to perfect rest and peace; but he knew that these were impossible so long as their sin was unconfessed and unforgiven. But it had now been abundantly confessed. Then, too, he had been anxious to see how they felt toward Benjamin. With this object in view he had given him five times as much as he had given them. Some think that he did this to show his special love. It may have been so; but probably there was something deeper. It was his dream of superiority that aroused their hatred against himself: how would they feel toward Benjamin, if he, the younger, were treated better than them all? But notwithstanding the marked favour shown him, they were as eager as before for his return with them. Besides, he wanted to see if they could forgive. It was Benjamin who had brought them into all this trouble: had they treated him in the spirit of former days, they would have abandoned him to his fate; but if so, they could not have been forgiven. "If ye forgive not men their trespasses, neither will your Heavenly Father forgive you." But they had no malice against this young lad. So far from showing malice, they tenderly loved and clung to him for the old father's sake and his own. Evidently then all Joseph's purposes were accomplished; all the conditions were fulfilled; and nothing remained to hinder the great unveiling that was so near.

III. Notice the Revelation and Reconciliation.

"Then Joseph could not refrain himself." There was no effort needed to bring himself to the point: the effort consisted in having restrained himself so long. If he had yielded to his natural feelings, he would have broken out long before. It was only because he studied their lasting welfare, that he refrained himself so long. But when Judah's voice ceased its pathetic pleading, he could restrain himself no more. It may be that some one will read this who has been disposed to think that our Saviour is hard to please; needing so much ere He unbends; distant and reticent. Ah, it is the other way! He is gentle and easy to be entreated; He is brimming over with yearning love: and if He seem indifferent, it is not for want of love—it is indeed a positive effort to Him even to seem so; and He will go through with it in order to prove, and test, and teach us. He loved the dear inmates of the home in Bethany, but He refrained Himself, and abode two days still in the same place where He was, so that Lazarus died; and then He went that He might work his greatest miracle at the grave in which hope itself lay buried. Whilst we are being tried, He will invite us to his table, and speak some words of love; yet there will be a veil between us: but when the trial is over, He will refrain Himself no more, but will manifest Himself to us as He does not unto the world. "His going forth is prepared as the morning."

And Joseph cried, "Cause every man to go out from me." There was great delicacy here. He did not want to expose his brethren; and yet he wanted to say words which could not be understood by the curious ears of mere courtiers and place-seekers. His brethren, too, must have a chance to be themselves. "And so there stood no man with him, while Joseph made himself known unto his brethren." We must stand alone before Christ, if we would know Him. The priest, the minister, or the Christian friend, must alike go out. There are joys, as there are sorrows, in which no stranger can intermeddle. As Peter met our Lord alone on the resurrection morning, for "He

was seen of Cephas"—so alone must each man meet Christ.
Why not at once?

And he wept aloud. He gave forth his voice in weeping, so
that the Egyptians heard the unusual sounds and wondered.
Was this joy or grief? I am disposed to think it was neither.
It was pent-up emotion. For many days he had been in suspense; so anxious not to lose them, so afraid that they might
not stand the test. When from some secret coign of vantage
he had watched them leave the city in the grey light, he may
have chided himself for letting them go at all. His mind had
been on the stretch; and now that the tension was removed,
and that there was no further necessity for it, he wept aloud.
Ah, sinner, the heart of Christ is on the stretch for thee!

And he said, "I am Joseph." He spoke in deep emotion;
yet the words must have fallen on them like a thunderbolt.
"Joseph!" Had they been dealing all the while with their long-
lost brother? "Joseph!" Then they had fallen into a lion's
den indeed. "Joseph!" Could it be? Yes, it must be so; and
it would explain a great many things which had sorely puzzled
them. Well might they be troubled and terrified. Astonishment
as at one risen from the dead, terror for the consequences, fear
lest he would repay them the long-standing debt—all these
emotions made them dumb. They could not answer him. So
he said again, "I am Joseph, *your brother,* whom ye sold into
Egypt"; and he added very lovingly, "Be not grieved, nor
angry, for God did send me." How much this reminds us of
another scene, not far from the gates of Damascus, when Jesus
arrested the young persecutor with the words, "Saul, why
persecutest thou Me?" And he said, "Who art Thou, Lord?"
And the answer came back, "I am Jesus, whom thou persecutest." Penitent sinner! it is thus that thy Saviour speaks to
thee. "I am Jesus, your brother, whom thou hast sold and
crucified; yet grieve not for that. I was delivered by the determinate counsel and fore-knowledge of God; though the hands
have been none the less wicked by whom I have been crucified
and slain. But if you repent, your sins shall be blotted out.

All manner of sin shall be forgiven unto the sons of men, and the blasphemies wherewith soever they may have blasphemed."

"*And Joseph said unto his brethren, Come near unto me.*" They had gone farther and farther back from him; but now he bids them approach. This is a beautiful illustration of the way in which a sinner may be reinstated in the loving favour of God. We are not set to serve a time of probation. We need not stand afar off. We may step right into the deepest and closest intimacy with the Son of God. Once "far off," but now "made nigh" by the blood of Jesus. One moment the rugged road of repentance; the next the Father's kiss and the banquet in the Father's home.

A moment more saw him and Benjamin locked in each other's arms, their tears freely flowing. And he kissed *all* his *brethren*. Simeon? Yes. Reuben? Yes. Those who had tied his hands and mocked his cries? Yes. He kissed them *all*. And after that they talked with him. So shall it be one day. The Jews are slowly filtering back to Palestine in unbelief. Sore troubles await them there, to prepare them to recognize their rejected Messiah. But the time is not far distant when they shall be prepared to hear Him say, "I am Jesus, your brother, whom ye crucified; but be not grieved with yourselves, for God has brought good out of evil, both for Gentile and for Jew, by saving life with a great deliverance." "And they shall look upon Him whom they pierced, and mourn because of Him." "And so all Israel shall be saved."

X

Joseph's Administration of Egypt
(Genesis xlvii)

"We see him as he moved,
How modest, kindly, all-accomplished, wise,
With what sublime repression of himself,
And in what limits, and how tenderly."
TENNYSON.

WHILE all the domestic details on which we have been meditating were transpiring, Joseph was carrying his adopted country through a great crisis—I might almost call it a revolution. When he became Prime Minister, the Egyptian monarchy was comparatively weak; but after he had administered affairs for some thirteen years, Pharaoh was absolute owner of all the land of Egypt. As it was in England in the old feudal times, so it was in Egypt: all the land became held in fief from the crown. The history of this change deserves more attention than we can give it now; but from first to last it was due to the statesmanship of the young Hebrew. Nor is this the only instance of a Hebrew conducting his adopted country through extraordinary perils by the exercise of extraordinary genius.

During the seven years of plenty, Joseph caused one-fifth of all the produce of every district to be hoarded up in its town; so that each town would contain, within immense granaries, the redundant produce of its own district. At last the years of famine came. And recent sad experiences in India will help us to realize something of the meaning of the words: "There was no bread in all the land, for the famine was very sore; so that the land of Egypt, and all the land of Canaan, fainted by reason of the famine." No doubt, had there been no provision made by Joseph, the streets would have been filled by emaciated skeletons picking their way feebly amid the heaps of the dying and the dead; men, women, and children would have fallen before the scythe of famine-fever; and it would have taken years for the country to be repopulated to its former extent.

The slender stores of the Egyptians were soon exhausted; and when all the land of Egypt was famished, the people cried unto Pharaoh, saying: "Bread! bread! give us bread!" Did they invade the palace precincts, flow into the corridors, and force their way into the royal presence, as the Parisian mob has done more than once in the awful days of revolution? We do not know. But Pharaoh had a ready answer: "Go unto Joseph; and what *he* saith unto you, do." "Then Joseph opened all the storehouses and *sold* unto the Egyptians." This was right and wise. It would have been a great mistake to *give*. In the Irish famine the Government set the people to earn their bread by making the roads, since it would have done them lasting injury to have allowed them to receive help without rendering some kind of equivalent. And it is not too much to say that it would have taken the Egyptians one or two generations to recover their moral tone if, instead of selling, Joseph had given the corn. Joseph's policy was in exact accord with the maxims of modern political economy.

But the money was soon exhausted: it lasted just one year. What was to be done now? There was nothing left but persons and lands; the people were naturally loth to pledge these, but there was no alternative; and so they came to Joseph, and said, "Why should we die? Buy us and our land for bread." In other words, they became Pharaoh's tenant farmers, and paid him twenty per cent, or one-fifth of their returns, as rent. This may seem a heavy tax; but it is not heavier than the rentage in almost every European country in the present day.

I. LET US STUDY THE SPIRIT OF JOSEPH'S ADMINISTRATION. It is summed up in three brief sentences: He was "diligent in business, fervent in spirit, serving the Lord."

Of his *diligence in business* there is ample proof. When first raised to the proud position of Premier, "he went out through all the land of Egypt." The granaries were built and the corn stored under his personal supervision. And when the famine came, the corn was sold under his own eye. The whole pressure of arrangements seems to have rested entirely upon his shoulders. Pharaoh wiped his hands of it, and said, Go to Joseph. Joseph gathered up all the money that was found in all the land of Egypt. Joseph bought the whole land for Pharaoh; and Joseph superintended the removal of the people into the cities from one end of the country to the other for the easier distribution of food. Joseph made the laws. "Seest thou a man diligent in his business, he shall stand before kings, he shall not stand before mean men." Young men, make Joseph your model in this. Some men do their lifework as if every joint were stiff with rheumatism, or as if they were exuding some adhesive viscus, making their snail progress as painful as it is slow. Others are somnambulists, looking for something and forgetting what they seek; not able to find their work, or, having found it, not able to find their tools; always late, taking their passage when the ship has sailed; insuring their furniture when the house is in flames; locking the door when the horse is gone. Beware of imitating any of these. First choose a pursuit, however humble, into which you can rightly throw your energy, and then put into it all your forces without stint.

These are simple rules, but most important. *Make the most of your time.* The biggest fortunes that the world has seen were made by saving what other men fling away; so be miserly over the moments, and redeem the gold-dust of time, and they will make a golden fortune of leisure. *Be punctual.* Some men are always out of step with old Father Time. They do not miss their appointments; but they always arrive five minutes late.

It would seem as if they were born late, and have never been able to catch up their lost moments. *Be methodical.* Arrange, so far as you can, your daily work, as postmen do their letters, in streets and districts; subject always, of course, to those special calls which the Almighty may put in your way. *Be prompt.* If your work must be done, do it at once: well-earned rest is sweet. *Be energetic.* An admirer of Thomas Carlyle met him once in Hyde Park, and broke in upon his reverie with an earnest request for a motto. The old man stood still for a moment, and then said, "There is no better motto for a young man than the words of the old book: 'Whatsoever thy hand findeth to do, do it with thy might.'"

But Joseph was also *fervent in spirit.* "He was a fruitful bough by a well, whose branches ran over the wall." It is almost impossible to exaggerate the beauty of this similitude. Yonder is the scorched land. You dare not expect verdure, much less fruit. Suddenly you descry greenery, and far-reaching boughs laden with luscious grapes. Why? Ah! down there lies a deep, deep well, and the rootlets of the vine go down into those cool depths, and draw up a moisture which the torrid heat cannot exhaust. Joseph's life was spent in a dry and thirsty land; here was not much in Egypt to nourish his spiritual life, yet to its close he bore fruit, which refreshed man and pleased God. Love, joy, peace, long-suffering, meekness, goodness, self-control, all these were in him even to abounding. And it was, no doubt, owing to his fervour of heart. It is related of a Grand Vizier, who in early life had been a shepherd, that he set apart one room in his palace for his exclusive use. No one was permitted to enter it. It was filled with the simple furniture of his early home, and the implements of his humble calling. And he entered it each day for quiet meditation on what he had been, that he might not be proud. So, surely, in Joseph's palace there was a retired room, where he spent many hours each week in communion with the God of his fathers, to whom he owed everything he had.

Would that more of our business men were "fervent in spirit"! There is too little of this. Time for the ledger, but none for the Bible. Time for the club or society, but none for the prayer-meeting. Time for converse with friends, but none for God. And, as the result, the bloom soon passes off the spirit, and the light dies away from the eyes, and the elasticity from the step. Men get to look wearied, tired, restless, and dissatisfied. Life bears a sombre aspect. And men in this condition are not able to refresh weary souls that pass hard by, searching in vain for the rich clusters of refreshing fruit. We cannot produce fruit by any efforts of our own. We can only be fruitful by sending our rootlets down to the well. We must make time for private prayer and for the loving study of the Bible. Then the glow of fervour would never die down in the heart; and the leaf would never look sere; and seasonable fruit would never be wanting. Think not that fervour of spirit is impossible to those who live amid the stir of business. It was not impossible to Joseph: it need not be impossible to any who will adopt the simple rules of the Bible and of common sense. It is not enough to light a fire—we must feed it. And yet how many of my readers may have gradually sunk into habits of carelessness in private devotion, such as are bound to reduce and extinguish fervour of soul! There is the well of God's own word! Get near it; strike deep into it; draw up from it by loving habitual study. Thus shall you be able to resist the insidious agencies that would drain away your enthusiasm and your power.

But Joseph was also a *servant of God*. God was in all his thoughts. "I fear God," was his motto. "It was not you that sent me hither, but God; and *He* hath made me . . . ruler throughout all the land of Egypt": this was the inspiration of his life. In saying that, he showed that he felt accountable to God for all he was and did. Now we surely need a principle to bind together our daily life and our religious exercises. So many live in business on one set of principles—and put on another set with their Sunday clothes. Where is the principle that will bring all our life beneath one blessed rule? I know of no other principle than that laid down by the good centurion, when he said, "A man under authority." We must feel hour by hour that we are men and women under the authority of the Lord Jesus Christ. The law of gravitation rules the sweep of the planets round the sun, and the course of a grain of dust in the autumn breeze. So obedience in everything to our Saviour will simplify and regulate all things, and reduce the chaos of our life to one symmetrical and beautiful whole. If there is anything in your life, any habit, any dress, any pursuit, which Christ cannot approve, it must be laid aside. His name must be written upon all the bells of life, or they must cease to ring. The Apostle invested with new dignity the existence of the poor slaves of his time, by saying, "Ye are servants of Christ: do service with a will, not as unto men, but as unto Christ." And it is of no consequence how menial your position is, you may do it for your dear Lord, whispering again and again, "This is for Thee, gracious Master, all for Thee." What a check this would put on hurried and superficial work!

There are a good many unfaithful servants about in the world; and if you rebuke them, you receive as answer, "My wages are so poor"; "My mistress takes no interest in me"; "I am treated as a slave"; "I shall leave as soon as I can." Stop! Who put you where you are? Had Christ anything to do with it? If not, how came you there without asking his leave? If He had, how dare you leave unless you are sure He calls you away? And as for service—why do you serve? For money, or thanks, or habit? No, *for Christ.* Then do your best for Him. Every room you enter is a room in his temple. Every vessel you touch is as holy as the vessels of the Last Supper. Every act is as closely noticed by Him as the breaking of the alabaster box. On every fragment of your life you may write, "Sacred to the memory of Jesus Christ." This would give a new dignity to toil, and a new meaning to life. Let us never forget how the thought of our dear Lord will equalize all life, and act as the complement of its needs. Those who are called as free, are slaves to Him; and those who are slaves to men are free in Him. And all life reaches its true unity and ideal just in so far as He is its Head, and Lord (1 Cor. vii. 22).

II. Notice the Confession of the Egyptians. "Thou hast saved our lives" (Gen. xlvii. 25). What a splendid endowment is coolness, foresight, presence of mind! They are the gift of God; and they have enabled many men to be the saviours of their fellows. That engineer had it who, some time ago, turned off the steam from the broken cylinder on the ocean steamer that seemed doomed. Livingstone and Stanley have had it among travellers; and it often saved them and their followers from infuriated mobs of savages. Cromwell and Wellington had it among soldiers, and it enabled them to extricate their men from positions in which death seemed certain. Cavour, Pitt, and Bright have had it pre-eminently among statesmen. Any of these might have been addressed in the words of the Egyptians: "Thou hast saved our lives."

But there is something higher than this. As I see these Egyptians crowding round Joseph with these words upon their lips, it makes me think of Him of whom Joseph was but a type. Joseph lay in the pit; and from the pit was raised to give bread to the brethren who had rejected him, and to a nation of Gentiles. Jesus lay in the grave; and from its dark abyss He was raised to give salvation to his brethren the Jews, and to the millions of Gentile people. Already I hear the sound of countless myriads, as they fall before the sapphire throne, and cry, "Thou hast saved us!" The Egyptian name of Joseph meant, "the Saviour of the world"; but the salvation wrought by him is hardly to be named in the same breath with that which Jesus has achieved. Joseph saved Egypt by sagacity; Jesus saved us by laying down his life. Joseph's bread cost him nothing; but the bread which Jesus gives cost Him Calvary. Joseph was well repaid by money, cattle, and land; but Jesus takes his wares to the market of the poor, and sells them to those who have no money or price. He can supply all our need. His only condition is that He should do it freely. To offer Him anything in exchange is to close all dealings with Him. But if you are willing to go without gold in your hand, and with an empty sack, He will give without stint, with both hands, pressed down, and running over. "He will fill the hungry with good things; but the rich He will send empty away." "Blessed are ye poor, for yours is the kingdom of heaven."

III. REMARK THE RESOLVE OF THESE EGYPTIANS. "Let us find grace; and we will be Pharaoh's servants." "Thou hast saved our lives; and we will be thy servants." How could we state better the great argument for our consecration to our Saviour? "He has saved us: ought we not to be his servants?"

There are many arguments by which we might urge acceptance of the yoke of Christ. There is such *dignity* in it: the old butler is proud to wear the livery of a ducal house; but what livery is so worthy as that which Christ's servants wear? "I bear the marks of the Lord Jesus." There is such *happiness* in it; it is perfect freedom. To be free of Christ is to grind in slavery. To obey Christ—is to go forth into the glorious liberty of the sons of God.

But I pass by these arguments now to present one more cogent, more pathetic, more moving. It is this: Jesus has saved you—will you not serve Him? These are the successive steps: mark them well! Recognize that Jesus bought you to be his by shedding his own blood as your ransom-price, and by giving his flesh for you and for the life of the world. Then give yourself entirely to Him, saying, humbly, lovingly, trustfully, "I do now, and here, offer a present unto Thee, O Lord, myself, my soul and body, to be a reasonable, holy, and lively sacrifice to Thee." From that moment you are no more your own, but his; He takes what we yield, at the moment of yielding; reckon on Him to keep you, and to supply all your need. Take Jesus to be moment by moment your Saviour, Friend, and Lord; and yield to Him an obedience which shall cover the entire area of your being, and shall comprehend every second of your time. When solicited to leave Him, appropriate the words of the ancient Hebrew slave, and say, "I love my Master; I will not go out free."

He deserves this. For you He lay in Bethlehem's manger. For you He was homeless and poor. For you He sweat the drops of blood and poured out his soul unto death. For you He pleads in heaven. "I beseech you then, by the mercies of God, that ye present yourselves to Him, living sacrifices, which is your reasonable service."

XI

JOSEPH'S FATHER
(GENESIS XLVII. 1–11)

"We live in deeds, not years; in thoughts, not breaths;
In feelings, not in figures on a dial;
We should count time by heart's throbs. He most lives
Who thinks most, feels the noblest, acts the best."
                                              P. J. BAILEY.

WE always turn with interest from an illustrious man to ask about his father and his mother. The father of Martin Luther and the mother of the Wesleys hang as familiar portraits in the picture-gallery of our fancy. It is not, therefore, to be wondered at that we find in the Bible something to gratify this innocent curiosity; and especially in the story of Joseph we are permitted to glance behind the scenes, and to consider the relations between him and his old father, Jacob.

I. JOSEPH'S UNDIMINISHED FILIAL LOVE. From the first moment that Joseph saw his brethren among the crowd of all nationalities that gathered in the corn-mart, it was evident that his love to his father burnt with undiminished fervour. Those brethren little guessed how eager he was to learn if the old man was yet alive, nor what a thrill of comfort shot through his heart when they happened to say, "Behold, our youngest brother is this day with his father." Evidently, then, though twenty-five years had passed since he beheld that shrunken, limping, yet beloved form, his father was living still.

And when his brethren came the second time, they must have been surprised to notice the delicate tenderness with which he asked them of their welfare, and said, "Is your father well, the old man of whom ye spake? is he yet alive?" Yes; and Judah little realized what a tender chord he struck, and how it vibrated, almost beyond endurance, to his touch, when he spoke again and again of the father at home, an old man, who so tenderly loved the young lad, the only memorial of his mother: that father who had been so anxious lest mischief should befall him; and whose grey hairs would go down with sorrow to the grave, unless he came back safe. It was this repeated allusion to his father that wrought on Joseph's feelings so greatly as to break him down. "He could not refrain himself." And so the very next thing he said, after the astounding announcement, "I am Joseph," was, "Doth my father yet live?" And in the tumultuous words which followed, words throbbing with passion and pathos, sentences about the absent father came rolling out along with utterances of reconciliation and forgiveness to his brethen: just as the swollen mountain flood hurries along in its eddies, boulders, timber, and everything that barred the way. "Haste ye, and go up to my father, and say unto him: Thus saith thy son Joseph, 'God hath made me lord of all Egypt: come down unto me; tarry not.' . . . And ye shall tell my father of all my glory in Egypt, and of all that ye have seen; and ye shall haste, and bring down my father hither."

The weeks and months that intervened must have been full of feverish anxiety to Joseph; and when at last he heard that the old man had reached the frontier of Egypt, in one of the waggons which, with thoughtful consideration, he had sent to fetch him, he "made ready his chariot, and went up to meet Israel his father." Oh, that meeting! If the old man was sitting in some recess of the lumbering wain, weary with the long journey, how he would revive when they said "Joseph is coming"! I think he would surely dismount, and wait, straining his aged eyes at the approaching company, from out the midst of which there came the bejewelled ruler to fall on his neck and weep there a good while. "Let me die," said he, as he looked at him, from head to foot with glad, proud, satisfied eyes: "Let me die, since I have seen thy face; because thou art yet alive." I wonder how he felt, as he recalled his sad lament, "All these things are against me."

But this was not all. Joseph loved his father too well to be ashamed of him. When Pharaoh heard of the arrival of his father and brethren, he seemed mightily pleased, and he directed Joseph to see to their welfare. "The land of Egypt is before thee; in the best of the land make thy father and brethren to dwell; in the land of Goshen let them dwell: and if thou knowest any men of activity among them, then let them be rulers over my cattle." After this Joseph brought in Jacob his father, and set him before Pharaoh.

We cannot but admire the noble frankness with which Joseph introduced his father to the splendid monarch, habituated to the manners of the foremost court of the world. There was a great social gulf fixed between Egypt and Canaan, the court and the tent, the monarch and the shepherd. And if Joseph had been any less noble or simple than he was, he might have shrunk from bringing the two extremes together; might have feared to recall the comparative lowliness of his origin; might have been ashamed of his relations, who needed to become pensioners on the land of his adoption. But all these thoughts were forgotten in presence of another: this withered, halting, famine-pursued man was *his father.*

There is a great laxity in these respects in all classes of our community, but especially among the children of working men in large industrial towns. The young people are able to earn such good wages as to be largely independent of their parents. And when they have paid some small amount for their keep, they are apt to imagine that their parents have no further claim. They forget the long arrears of obligation. They do not care to remember the cost of those long years of helpless childhood, when they were only a burden and a care. They are unmindful of the tender kindness that nursed them through long and dangerous illnesses; that freely sacrificed sleep and rest; that thought them angels, saints, and heroes; that bore with their petulance and fretfulness; or that sat far into the night, contriving dresses, playthings, and other pleasant surprises.

In some cases the behaviour of grown-up children to their parents is still more dishonourable. It is a common thing to see men rise in a few years from obscurity to considerable wealth. With increasing money there comes a vast change in a man's social position. He puts the magic letters "Esq." after his name. He lives in a fine house, and gives large parties. He keeps his carriage, and sends his children to expensive schools. But what of his aged parents? He allows them a meagre annuity; but takes care to keep them out of his family and his home—for, to tell the truth, he is rather ashamed of them. It is a false shame indeed! And the man who does so is almost certain, unconsciously, to say or do something which will reveal to his new associates his lowly origin far more readily than the mere presence of his parents at his board could do. I prefer the noble magnanimity of Joseph, who seemed proud to introduce the withered, crippled patriarch to his mighty friend and liege lord.

Young people, honour your parents! Do not treat them the worse, just because you know they love you enough to bear with your impertinences. The politeness is mere veneer which is not gentle to near kin. Do not call them by slang or unmeaning names: glory in the noble titles, "Father," "Mother." They may have their peculiarities and faults; but it is ungenerous and unkind to dwell on them. It is possible so to fix your attention on these minor points as to become oblivious to many noble qualities, which are more than a compensation. Imitate the sons of Noah in the filial respect which flung a mantle even over their father's sin.

II. PHARAOH'S QUESTION. "How old art thou?" This was Pharaoh's first inquiry, as Jacob entered his presence. It was, perhaps, suggested by the patriarch's withered look and bent form. It is a question that often rises to our lips; but it is suggested by a very false standard of estimating the length of a man's life.

The length of a life is not measured by the number of its days; no, but by the way in which its days have been used.

> "*We live in thoughts, not breaths;*
> *In feelings, not in figures on a dial.*"

Some live for many years, and at the end have little or nothing to show for them. Take out the wasted hours, hours of drowsy lethargy, hours of luxurious sloth, and hours of self-indulgence; and only a few hours of real life are left. There are men who will be seventy next birthday, but who have only lived six months out of the whole time. It is surprising in Liverpool to see the great bales of cotton compressed under the vast pressure of the hydraulic press; and so lives shrink into a very insignificant space, beneath the mighty pressure of reality. Our real life dates, not from our first birth, but from our second. All before that counts for nothing.

Others live for few years, but they have crowded them with strenuous, noble life: they have been punctual, industrious, methodical: they have redeemed the time; they have treasured the moments with frugal and miserly care; they have made the most of odd bits which others would have flung away as useless—and, as the result, they have much to show. What books they have read! What deeds they have done! What ministries they have set afoot! What friends they have made! What characters they have built up! They have lived long. They will be thirty next birthday; but in those few years they have lived the life which most men live in sixty years.

Permit a stranger to ask of each reader, standing in the palace of life, "How old art thou?"

How old art thou? *Seventeen?* That is indeed a critical time. It is the formative time: what thou art now, thou wilt be. Thou art leaving the sheltered bay of early life to launch out into the great ocean. Beware! it is winsome-looking, but it is treacherous. Be sure and take on board the great Master, Christ: none but He can pilot thee through the shoals and quicksands which lie hidden on thy course. Take on board none but those whom He chooses as the crew.

How old art thou? *Twenty-one?* That is often described as the time of a man's majority, or independence. Never forget that there is at least One of whom thou canst never be independent. Thou mayest disown Him, and go into a far country to waste his substance and thine own in riotous living; but thou wilt have to come back to Him at last. There is no true rest, or food, or honour, outside his palace-home. Prodigal child, come home! Come home!

How old art thou? *Thirty?* It was at that age that our Lord emerged from obscurity: and think how many men have lived a great life and died before they reached this age. Alexander among generals; Kirke White among singers; McCheyne and Spencer among ministers. What art thou doing in the world? Come, make haste! Thy life will soon slip away. Take care, lest at the close thou be constrained to say, "I have spent my life in laboriously doing trifles."

> " 'Tis a mournful story,
> Thus in the ear of pensive eve to tell
> Of morning's firm resolves the vanished glory,
> Hope's honey left within the with'ring bell,
> And plants of mercy dead, that might have bloomed so well."

But this need not be your sad retrospect, if only you will yield your whole being to the Lord Jesus, asking Him to keep down your self-life, and to think in your brain, to live in your heart, to work through your life, and to fulfil in you the good pleasure of his will, "and the work of faith with power."

How old art thou? *Forty?* Take care! Very few are ever converted who have reached the downward slopes of forty. If thou art not Christ's yet, the chances of thy becoming his lessen at a tremendous ratio every week.

How old art thou? *Fifty? Sixty? Seventy?* The snows are beginning to silver thy head. Familiar pursuits must be abandoned. Familiar places must be visited no more. Affairs once thy pride must be given over to the stronger nerve of others. The dip in yonder path shows how near is the valley of the shadow of death, with its dark, dark river. How art thou going to meet it? Shivering, cringing, cowering, the victim of an irresistible fate? Or with brave welcome, such as animated the worn prisoner of the Mamertine dungeon? "I have fought a good fight, I have finished my course, I have kept the faith; henceforth there is laid up for me a crown of righteousness." Old friends, we look on you to teach us how to await our end, and how to die.

It is a solemn question, How old art thou? It is well to face the growing fewness of our years; to see how envious Time is eating away the narrow shoal on which we stand. My favourite piece in all Milton's works is his address to Time; and often have I loved to read the passage in Charles Kingsley's Life, which tells how on his dying bed he read it again and again—

"Fly, envious Time, till thou run out of race."

Oh to be able to say that without tremor or misgiving!

III. JACOB'S ANSWER. "And Jacob said unto Pharaoh, The days of the years of my pilgrimage are an hundred and thirty years; few and evil have the days of the years of my life been, and have not attained unto the days of the years of the life of my fathers in the days of their pilgrimage." They had been *few* in comparison with those of his ancestors. Terah reached the age of 205; Abraham of 175; Isaac of 180. But "the whole age of Jacob was an hundred forty and seven years." They had been *evil*. As a young man he was wrenched from his dearest associations of home and friends, and went forth alone to spend the best years of his life as a stranger in a strange land. Arduous and difficult was his service to Laban, consumed

in the day by drought, and in the sleepless night-vigils by
frost. He escaped from Laban with difficulty; and no sooner
had he done so than he had to encounter his incensed and
impetuous brother. In the agony of that dread crisis he met
with the Angel Wrestler, who touched the sinew of his thigh,
so that he halted to the end of his life. These calamities had
hardly passed when he was involved in extreme danger with
the Canaanites of Shechem, and passed through scenes which
have blanched his hair, furrowed his cheeks, and scarred his
heart. Thus he came to Luz, and Deborah, Rebekah's nurse,
died, and was buried beneath an oak, which was thenceforth
called the Oak of Weeping. "And they journeyed from Bethel,
and there was but a little way to come to Ephrath, and Rachel
(his favourite wife) bare a son; and it came to pass, as her soul
was departing, for she died, that she called his name Ben-oni,
the son of my sorrow." A little further on he came to Mamre,
arriving just in time to bear the remains of his own father to
the grave. And what sorrows befell him after that, have
already touched our hearts, as we have studied the wondrous
history of his son, Joseph. Reuben involved his name in shameful disgrace. Judah trailed the family honour in the mire of
sensual appetite. To all appearance Joseph had been torn to
pieces by wild beasts. The dissensions of his sons must have
rent his heart. And even after his meeting with his long-lost
son he was to linger for seventeen years a pensioner on the
bounty of the king of Egypt: far from the glorious heritage
which had been promised to his race.

Such was the exterior of Jacob's life. Few have trod a path
more paved with jagged flints, or bound around their brows a
crown more full of thorns. You would have called his life a
failure. Compare it with the lot of Esau; and what a contrast
it presents! Jacob obtained the birthright; but what a life of
suffering and disaster was his! Esau lost the birthright; but
he had all that heart could wish. Wealth, royalty, a line of
illustrious sons—these were the portion of his cup. The thirty-
sixth chapter of Genesis contains a list of the royal dukes of

his line. How often must Esau have pitied his brother! "My poor brother, he was always visionary, counting on the future, building castles in the air; as for myself, I say, make the best of this world while it lasts. Let us eat and drink, for to-morrow we may die."

And yet when this same Jacob stands before Pharaoh, the greatest monarch of the world bends eagerly to catch his blessing. "Jacob blessed Pharaoh." I know that Jacob in his earlier life was crafty, a mere bargain-maker, a trickster; but all seems to have been eliminated in the fierce crucible of suffering through which he had passed; and he had reached a grandeur or moral greatness which impressed even the haughty Pharaoh. Esau would never have been able to bless Pharaoh. But this way-worn pilgrim can now do that which his wealthy and successful brother never could have done. "Without contradiction, the less is blessed of the greater." Evidently, then, Jacob was a greater man than the greatest monarch of his time. There is, therefore, a greatness which is wholly independent of those adventitious circumstances which we sometimes associate with it. The ermine does not make a judge; a crown does not make a king; nor does wealth, or rank, or birth make a great man. Jacob was one of the truly great. He was a royal man with a Divine patent of royalty. God Himself said, "Thy name shall be no more called Jacob, but Israel (a prince of God), for as a prince hast thou power with God, and with men."

Three things made Jacob royal; and will do as much for us.

(1) *Prayer.* On the moorland, strewn with boulders, he saw in his dreams the mighty rocks pile themselves into a heaven-touching ladder. This struck the keynote of his life. He ever after lived at the foot of the ladder of prayer, up which the angels sped to carry his petitions, and down which they came, with beautiful feet, to bring the golden handfuls of blessing. Learn to pray without ceasing. It is the secret of greatness. He who is oft in the audience-chamber of the great King becomes kinglike.

(2) *Suffering.* His nature was marred by selfish, base, and

carnal elements. He took unlawful advantage of his famished brother; deceived his aged father; increased his property at the expense of his uncle; worked his ends by mean and crafty means. But sorrow ate away all these things, and gave him a new dignity. So does it work still on those who have received the new nature, and who meekly learn the lesson which God's love designs to teach them. Do not shrink from pain and sorrow; they come to crown you. The Lamb sits on the throne to-day because He was slain; and the throne is reserved for those who have learnt to suffer with Him, and with Him to die.

(3) *Contact with Christ.* "There wrestled a man with him until the breaking of the day." Who was He? Surely none less than the Angel Jehovah, whose face may not be seen, or his name known. It was the Lord Himself, anticipating his incarnation, and intent on ridding his servant of the evil and weakness which had clung so long and so closely to him, sapping his spiritual life. And from that hour Jacob was "Israel." Ah, my readers, be sure of this, that Jesus, the immortal lover of souls, is wrestling with you, longing to rid you of littleness and selfishness, and to lift you also to a royal life. Yield to Him, lest He be compelled to touch the sinew of your strength. If you let Him have his way, He will make you truly Princes with God; and even those above you in this world's rank will gladly gather round you for the sake of the spiritual blessings you shall bestow.

XII

JOSEPH AT THE DEATH-BED OF JACOB
(GENESIS XLVII. 27–31)

"This hath He done; and shall we not adore Him?
This shall He do; and can we still despair?
Come, let us quickly fling ourselves before Him,
Cast at His feet the burden of our care.

"Yea, thro' life, death, thro' sorrow, and thro' sinning,
He shall suffice me, for He hath sufficed:
Christ is the end—for Christ was the beginning;
Christ the beginning—for the end is Christ."
F. W. H. MYERS.

JACOB dwelt in the land of Goshen; there his sons led their flocks over the rich pasture-lands, and laid the foundation of the great wealth which has ever been a distinguishing mark of this highly-favoured nation. "They grew and multi-plied exceedingly." So seventeen uneventful years went by. And as the old man became more and more infirm, his spirit was cheered and sustained by the love of Joseph, and by the satisfied joy of his heart in the honour and splen-dour of his son. Evidently Joseph was the stay of that waning life; and it is not remarkable therefore that the patriarch summoned him not once, or even twice, but thrice, to his death-bed. It is on those visits that we may dwell for a little now.

Evidently there is something to repay us. The Bible is a book of life. Its pages are devoted to the deeds rather than the deaths of its heroes. Their biographies fill whole books, whilst single verses are enough for their dying words. When-

ever, therefore, a death-scene is described with some minuteness, we may be sure that there is something which demands
our attentive heed. So it is here.

I. JOSEPH'S FIRST VISIT.—"The time drew nigh that Israel
must die." How inexorable is the "must" of death! There
is no possibility of evading its summons. When it lays its long,
cold hand on the shoulder of the Ancient Mariner, however
eager the guests to hear his story, he must arise and follow.
By many years had Jacob exceeded the ordinary span of
modern life; and, in spite of much hardship and privation, like
the apple at the extremity of the bough, which eludes the hand
of the gatherer, he had evaded the reach of death; but this
could not be for ever. The failing powers of his life gave
warning that the silver cord was strained to breaking, and
that the machinery of nature was on the point of giving way.
He must die.

But his death was a rift in the dark clouds that veiled the
future world from his sons and their children, giving them a
glimpse of its reality and beauty. And we can gather some
of the conceptions which must have flashed across the mind
of Joseph, as he obeyed the summons of his father, and stood
beside that dying bed.

One of the most sublime verses in the New Testament
declares that "Christ has abolished death, and brought life and
immortality to light through the Gospel." There is a most
inspiring rhythm in the words; but we must not suppose that
the Gospel has revealed that concerning which nothing was
previously known. Long before our Lord walked this world,
carrying at his girdle the keys of Resurrection and Life, men
cherished the hope of eternal life: the Gospel simply threw
fuller light on that which had been before partially hidden,
as the rising sun reveals the clear outlines of the landscape
which had lain indistinct and hazy in the grey dawn. Christ
drew from the window the curtain, through which the morning
light had been feebly struggling to the sleeper's eyes.

The evidence of this is not far to seek. Daniel teaches in plainest language the truth of a general resurrection to endless life or endless shame. Ecclesiastes closes with an explicit statement of the spirit's return to its giver, and of final judgment. The book of Job, whatever date may be assigned to it, has been called a very hymn of immortality: he knew at least that his "Redeemer lived, and that he should stand up at the last upon the earth, and after his skin had been destroyed, yet from his flesh he should see God" (Job xix. 25, 26, R.V.). In the Book of Psalms we have no uncertain evidence of the tenacity with which pious Jews clung to these hopes. "Thou wilt not leave my soul in sheol; neither wilt thou suffer thine Holy One to see corruption. Thou wilt show me the path of life" (Ps. xvi. 10, 11, R.V.). And it is just this faith in and yearning after a life beyond the grave which is the true key-note of the lives of the three great patriarchs who lie together in Machpelah's ancient cave.

Why did they wander to and fro in the land of promise as sojourners in a strange land? Why were they content to have no inheritance—no, not so much as a place to put their feet on? Why did Abraham dwell with Isaac and Jacob in frail, shifting tents, rather than in towns like Sodom and Gomorrah? What did Abraham mean when he said to the sons of Heth, "I am a stranger and a sojourner with you"? And what was the thought in Jacob's mind, when, in the presence of the haughty Pharaoh, he described his life as a "pilgrimage"? The answer is clearly given in the roll-call of God's heroes contained in Hebrews xi.: "They sought a country, a fatherland." And they were so absorbed with this one thought, that they could not settle to any inheritance in Canaan. Their refusal to have anything more than a grave in the soil of the promised land shows how eagerly they looked for the land that was very far off.

At first, no doubt, they thought that Canaan was to be the land of promise. But when they waited for it year after year, and still it was withheld, they looked into the deed of gift again, and learned that there were depths in it of which they had never dreamed; and as they still watched and waited, the gauzy mists of time parted, and in the dim haze there loomed upon their vision a land of which the land of milk and honey was a poor type; and instead of a city built by human hands, there arose before them the fair vision of the crystal walls and the pearly gates of the city which hath foundations, whose builder and maker is God, and which He hath prepared for them that love Him. Yonder was their fatherland. Yonder their true city. Yonder their home. And their pilgrim-life bore evidence to the reality and certainty of their faith.

This belief in "the city of God," of which in after-days Augustine wrote on the coast of Africa, and which has sustained so many saintly souls, animated their lives, cheered them in death, and cast a bright ray across the gloom of the grave. "These all died in faith, not having received the promises, but having seen them afar off (as the minarets and parapets of some distant city), and were persuaded of them and embraced them." The Revised Version says, "They greeted them from afar," as the wanderer greets his longed-for home, when he sees it from afar. With what eagerness, with what earnest yearnings, with what fond anticipation, must these weary wanderers have looked for heaven! Well might Jacob, on this his death-bed, stay the progress of his parting exhortations to say, "I have waited for thy salvation, O Lord." This took the bitterness out of his death.

And notice, *Jacob did not regard the future life as a mere state of existence* stript of all those associations which make life worth the having. Indeed, in this he seems to have had truer thoughts than many who are found in Christian churches. He said, "I am to be gathered unto my people." He surely did not mean simply that he was to be buried in their tomb, for he expresses that thought afterwards in the words, "Bury me with my fathers in the cave of Machpelah." Nay, he meant to say that for him the city to which he went was the gathering-place of his clan, the rendezvous of elect souls, the home of all who were *his* people because they were *God's*.

Year after year the people have been gathering there, as highland clans in olden days were gathered to a central trysting-place by the bearers of the Fiery Cross. All noble, saintly souls are assembled yonder, and await us. And when we leave this world, it will not be to go into a cold, unsympathizing, grave-like realm, where no voice shall greet, no smile welcome us. But we shall go to our people; those whom we have loved and lost; those who are awaiting our coming with fond affection, and who will administer a choral entrance to us into that world of everlasting re-union.

But it was not simply to express these hopes that the dying patriarch summoned the beloved Joseph to his side. The father wanted to bind the son by a solemn promise not to have him buried in the land of his exile, but to carry him back to that lone cave, which seemed an outpost in the hostile and distant land of Canaan. For seventeen years Jacob had been familiar with Egypt's splendid temples, obelisks, and pyramids; he had been surrounded with all the comforts that Joseph's filial love could devise or his munificence execute; but nothing could make him forget that distant cave, which was before Mamre, in the land of Canaan. To him interment in the most splendid pyramid in Egypt was not for a moment to be compared with burial in that solitary and humble sepulchre, where the mortal remains of Abraham and Sarah, of Isaac and Rebekah, and of the faithful Leah, lay waiting the day of resurrection.

Human nature was not different then from what it is to-day. Our truest home is still by the graves of the beloved dead. Wherever we wander, our hearts return thither, as the eye of the sailor to the Pole-star. And for this cause, many a warrior, dying in some distant land, has asked that his remains might be placed, not in the splendid Minster or the national Walhalla, but in the quiet country graveyard, where the moss-covered tombstones repeat in successive generations the family name. It was natural, then, for Jacob to wish to be buried in Machpelah.

But there was something more than natural sentiment. He was a man of faith. He knew and cherished the ancient promise made by God to His friend, the patriarch Abraham, that Canaan should become the possession of his seed. That promise was the old man's stay. He knew that Canaan and not Egypt was the destined abiding-place of his people. They would not always live in Egypt, however fertile its Goshens or friendly its peoples. The trumpet would sound the summons of their departure. If, then, he were buried in Egypt, he would be left behind, a stranger amongst strangers. No, this could not be. If they are to leave, he must leave before them. If they are to settle in the land of promise, he will go first as their forerunner. And though he could not share the perils and pains and glories of the exodus, he will be there to meet them when in after-years their bands enter upon their inheritance.

"If now I have found grace in thy sight, put, I pray thee, thy hand under my thigh, and deal kindly and truly with me. Bury me not, I pray thee, in Egypt: but I will lie with my fathers; and thou shalt carry me out of Egypt and bury me in their burying-place." What son could resist that appeal? Can any of us resist the last appeals of our beloved? Joseph was too good and tender to hesitate for a single moment. "And he said, I will do as thou hast said." But the old man was not content with a mere promise. "And he said, Swear unto me. And he sware unto him. And Israel bowed himself upon the bed's head." So ended Joseph's first visit to his dying father.

II. JOSEPH'S SECOND VISIT.—Tidings came to the Prime Minister of Egypt that his father was sick and wished to see him. And he went to him without delay, taking with him his two sons, Manasseh and Ephraim. He, no doubt, guessed that his father's sickness was the last stage of his decay; and the form of the message may have been agreed on by them in previous conversations as the significant sign from one to the other that the sands of time had nearly run out in that aged, battered, and time-worn body.

When Joseph arrived at his father's dwelling, the gift of his own munificence, the aged patriarch seems to have been lying still, with closed eyes, in the extreme of physical exhaustion. He was too weak to notice any of those familiar forms that stood around him. But when one told him and said, "Behold, thy son Joseph is come," the sound of that loved name revived him, and he made a great effort, and, propped by pillows, sat up upon the bed.

There was clearly no decay in his power of recollection, as the old man reviewed the past. Again he seemed to be lying at the foot of the mystic ladder, with its angels trooping up and down, whilst God Almighty stood above, and pledged Himself to make him fruitful, and to give to him and his seed the land in which his forefathers had been strangers, for an everlasting possession. No lapse of time could erase the impression which those words had made. Even though he had lived to out-measure the years of a Methuselah, they would still ring in musical cadence within his heart. And had not God fulfilled them a thousand times over, so that not one good thing had failed?—and his seed was sure of the land, though as yet far removed from its actual possession. And as his recollection embraced the past, it was also vividly alive to more recent incidents in the family history. He did not forget that Joseph, who leant over his dying form, had two sons; and he announced his intention of adopting them as his own. "Thy two sons, which were born unto thee in the land of Egypt, before I came unto thee into Egypt, are mine: as Reuben and Simeon, they shall be mine." By that act, whilst Joseph's name was expunged from the map of Canaan, yet he himself became possessed of a double portion of his area, because Ephraim and Manasseh would henceforth stand there as his representatives.

And when he had said so much, his mind wandered away. He saw again that scene on the hilly road to Bethlehem, just

outside the little village, where his onward progress was suddenly halted, and all his camp was hushed into the stillness of
a dread suspense, as the life of the beloved Rachel trembled
in the balance. He could never forget that moment. His dying
eyes could see again the spot where he buried her, "there in
the way of Ephrath."

> *"Be near me when all else is from me drifting,*
>   *Stars, sky, home-pictures, days of shade and shine,*
> *And kindly faces to my own uplifting,*
>   *The love that answers mine.*
>
> *"Suffice it, if my good and ill unreckoned,*
>   *And both forgiven by Thine abounding grace,*
> *I find myself by hands familiar beckoned,*
>   *Unto my fitting place."*
>
>   WHITTIER.

When the old man came back from his pathetic reverie, the
first sight which arrested him was the presence of the awe-
struck boys, who were drinking in every look and word, with
fixed and almost breathless heed.

"Who are these?" said Israel.

"They are my sons," was the proud and immediate reply,
"whom God hath given me in this place."

And Israel said, "Bring them, I pray thee, unto me, and I
will bless them."

And so they were brought near, and the aged lips were
pressed on the young foreheads, and the aged arms were put
feebly around the young and slender forms. And then again
the dying man wandered back to a grief which had left as deep
a scar as his sorrow for the beloved Rachel, and turning to
Joseph, he reminded him of the long years during which he
thought he would never look again upon his face. But now,
God, who may keep men waiting, but loves to fill their lives
ultimately with blessing, had shown him also his seed.

With prophetic insight he crossed his hands, as the two lads waited before him for his blessing, so that his right found its way to the head of the younger, whilst his left alighted on that of the elder. By that act he reversed the verdict of their birth, and gave the younger precedence over the elder. It was useless for Joseph to remonstrate, and to urge the claims of his first-born. The old man knew quite well what he was doing, and that he was on the line of the divine purpose. "I know it, my son, I know it; he also shall become a people, and he also shall be great: but truly his younger brother shall be greater than he, and his seed shall become a multitude of nations."

There was nothing arbitrary in this; for in all likelihood there were qualities in Ephraim, as afterwards in his descendants, which naturally put him in the foremost place. The Old Testament is full of hope for younger sons: Jacob was a younger son; so was Moses; so was Gideon; so was David. It is not an unmitigated blessing to be born into the world with a great name and estate and traditions; it is better to trust in one's own right arm and in the blessing of the Almighty. God is no respecter of persons, and He will lift the youngest into the front rank if only he sees the qualities which warrant it; whilst He will put back the foremost into the lower ranks if they are deficient in noble attributes. Thus the first become last, and the last first.

With hands crossed over the young heads the patriarch spoke sweet and grateful words of the Angel who had redeemed him from all evil; and his words are so chosen, and that name is so placed in parallelism with the name of God who had shepherded him all his life long, that we are convinced that he is speaking of the Angel-Jehovah, who is so often referred to on the pages of the Old Testament; and who can be no other than the Second Person of the ever-blessed Trinity, whose delights have always been with the sons of men, and who, before He took on Himself the form of a man, was often found in that of an angel.

We, too, have an Angel guardian, yea, *the* Angel, who is
Jesus Christ the Lord. If you want to be redeemed from all
evil, especially from the evil of sin, make much of Him. And
if He began his redemptive work long years before He suffered,
died, and rose, how much more will He do for us now that
He sits on the right hand of God! Take heart, you who are
anxious about your daily food. Listen to the testimony of this
dying man, that God had fed him all his life long unto that
day. And if God did so for a hundred and forty-seven years,
surely He will not forget you during the briefer span of your
few days.

There was one thing only more to say, before this memorable interview ended. Years before, Jacob had become em-
broiled through the dastardly treachery of his sons, in conflict
with the original inhabitants of Canaan, and had been compelled, in self-defence, to acquire by force a parcel of land,
with his sword and with his bow. *This* he gave as an additional
portion to his favourite son.

Would that all young persons who read these lines may so
act towards their parents that they may never give them an
anxious moment: that they may be their pride in life; their
stay in death: so that in after-years they may have the memory
of death-bed blessings, and may have nothing to regret! A
parent's dying blessing is a richer legacy than gold or lands.

III. JOSEPH'S THIRD AND LAST VISIT.—Once more Joseph
visited that death-chamber. This was the third time and the
last. But this time he stood only as one of twelve strong,
bearded men, who gathered around the aged form of their
father, his face shadowed by death, his spirit aglow with the
light of prophecy. How intense the awe with which they heard
their names called, one by one, by the old man's trembling
voice, now pausing for breath, now speaking with great difficulty! The character of each is criticized with prophetic insight; the salient points of their past history are vividly brought
to mind; and some fore-shadowing is given them of their future.

This scene is an anticipation of the Judgment-seat: where men shall hear the story of their lives passed under review; and a sentence passed, against which there shall be no appeal.

But the dying patriarch speaks with peculiar sweetness and grace, when he comes to touch on the destiny of his favourite son. His words brim with tenderness, and move with a stateliness and eloquence, which indicate how his heart was stirred to its depths. This was his swan-song, the final outburst of the music of his soul, the last flash of that Spirit of Inspiration, which dwelt also in him. What a glimpse is given to us into the depths of his soul; the secret thoughts of fruitfulness, patience, and strength, and the far-reaching conceptions of blessedness, which had been wrought out within him by the slow process of years of sorrow and training!

A few more sentences to Benjamin, and the venerable patriarch drew up his feet into his bed, and quietly breathed his last, and was gathered unto his people. But that eager, much-tried spirit passed up and away into other scenes of more exalted fellowship and ministry, with no pause in his life, for in after-years God attested his continued existence and energy when He called Himself "the God of Jacob", for God is not God of the dead, but of the living. And Joseph fell upon his father's face, and wept upon him, and pressed his warm lips on the death-cold clay; and he commanded the physicians to embalm his body, so cheating death of its immediate victory.

XIII

THE SECRET OF FRUITFULNESS
(GENESIS XLIX 22)

"Do I need here
To draw the lesson of this life: or say
More than these few words, following up the text:
The vine from every living limb bleeds wine,
Is it the poorer for that spirit shed?

.　　.　　.　　.　　.

Measure thy life by loss instead of gain;
Not by the wine drunk, but the wine poured forth;
For love's strength standeth in love's sacrifice;
And whoso suffers most hath most to give."
                    MRS. HAMILTON KING.

"A FRUITFUL bough by a well." Often had the eyes of the
dying man been refreshed by such a spectacle greeting him
amid wastes of sand—an oasis in the desert. For hours the
weary caravan has been pressing on, parched tongues cleaving
to the mouths, eyes scorching in the head, the strength of the
patient beasts and of the women and children almost giving
out. When, lo, the monotony of desert is broken by a welcome
sight! Over some grey crumbling stones a vine reaches out its
verdant and fruitful arms; and all press forward with redoubled
haste, knowing most surely that down beneath the rootlets
must be spreading themselves in dark, cool depths, where the
longed-for water is stored.

It will well repay us to go into the vinery, and talk with
some experienced vine-dresser of the growth of the vine, which
had been a familiar object with our blessed Lord from early

boyhood, and led Him to select the vine as the emblem of the union between Himself and those who believe. "I am the true Vine," said He, the Vine of which all others are parables and types. He might have chosen the summer corn, or the olive, or the forest tree; but He chose the vine, which clings, stretching out innumerable tendrils by which to hold and climb.

> *" And as it grows it is not free to heaven,*
> *But tied unto a stake; and if its arms stretch out*
> *It is but cross-wise, also forced and bound;*
> *And so it draws out of the hard hill-side,*
> *Fixed in its own place, its own food of life."*

Visit the vine in the late autumn, when its treasures have been torn from it. Whilst the land is full of joy it stands stripped and desolate. Its sap sinks down to the root; its branches are cut back to the stem; its very bark is peeled off; and it is left to the nipping of the merciless frost. Nothing more desolate and dismal can be conceived in plant-life than the death which reigns supreme over the vine through the long, lone winter. And as we contrast the glory of the spring with such desolation, we remember the words of Him who said, "Except a corn of wheat fall into the ground and die, it abideth alone; but if it die, it bringeth forth much fruit"; and how, outcast and forsaken, He hung upon the Cross, in what may well be said to have been the darkest, saddest hour of winter through which earth ever passed.

But when the sun leads back the spring, the sap begins to flow again; and beneath its impulse the branches start right and left from the long bare stems, and presently, when there is sun, flowers and the promise of fruit appear.

> *" The flower of the vine is but a little thing,*
> *The least part of its life. You scarce could tell*
> *It ever had a flower; the fruit begins*
> *Almost before the flower has had its day."*

Sunshine is essential. Without it the vine bears "nothing but leaves"—leaves in profusion, but leaves only. It is not enough for us to be connected by a living faith to Jesus: we must hold fellowship with Him, sunning ourselves in his smile, communing with Him, and surrendered to his companionship; so only can we hope to bear something more than the leaves of a mere profession.

But though the vine needs sunshine, *it must also have the darkness.* During the night it is said to rest: it does not grow; but it recuperates itself and prepares for the putting forth of fresh energy. During the day it consumes more sap than it can draw up from the root; and during the dark hours of night it is accumulating stores on which to feed. And this may suggest why sometimes after periods of much activity the great Husbandman draws down the blinds and plunges us into the black night of sorrow, or solitude, or depression. We have been too prodigal of our resources, and need time in order to recuperate our exhausted vigour, and to gather up stores for days to come.

The fruitfulness, however, of the vine largely depends on the care with which it is pruned. There is no tree pruned so mercilessly and incessantly, first with the sharp knife, and then with scissors. The Lord has many such implements. There is the *golden* pruning knife of his Word, by which He would prune us if we would let Him (John xv. 3), so escaping the rougher and more terrible discipline of the *iron* pruning knife of affliction. Our Lord uses the knife, with its sharp clean strokes, which cut deep into our nature, and leave scars which it will take years to heal, or even to conceal. And there are the scissors also in his hand—cross events, daily circumstances which appear contrary to each other, but which nevertheless work together in the end for good.

So great are the spring prunings that more branches are taken out than left in; and the cuttings which litter the ground are said to be utterly worthless and fit only for the fire. Apple and pear prunings are used in many ways, such as supports for young and frail plants; but not so these. And so there are many professors amongst us, who have neither part nor lot with us, who must be taken away; just as there are many things in us all which need pruning out. What a comfort it is that the Vine-dresser leaves the pruning to no 'prentice hand! The novice does anything but that. No hand but the most skilled may handle the knife. "My Father is the husbandman."

It is a recognized rule that no shoot should have more than one bunch of grapes. All but that one are nipped off. And I am told that the vine-dresser will obtain a greater weight of better grapes in that one bunch, than he would by permitting two or three clusters to form. And so with merciless hand he picks off bunch after bunch of unformed fruit and berry after berry from the reddening swelling cluster. It is thus that we are sometimes shut away from one after another of our chosen directions of Christian activity: not that our Father would diminish our fruit-bearing, but that the strength of our life may be saved from dissipation, and conducted by one channel to a better and richer fruitage.

How many pruned ones may read these words! They are inclined to say that the Lord hath dealt very bitterly with them. Husband and sons buried in a distant land; poverty and want supreme in a deserted and darkened home; only one left of all the merry circle of bygone years: and yet out of all this shall come a golden harvest of blessing; and the one little grandson pressed to the heart, and his line to David, the sweet Psalmist and mighty king, shall be better than seven sons, and shall make the aged heart young again. "No chastisement for the present seemeth to be joyous, but grievous: nevertheless afterward it yieldeth the peaceable fruit of righteousness unto them which are exercised thereby" (Ruth iv. 15; Heb. xii. 11).

It is very needful that the pruned branch should abide constantly in the vine. "Abide in Him!" (1 John ii. 28). This command was given first to *little children*. It was thus the beloved Apostle, whose head was silvered with many winters, wrote to young men and fathers, in the tender relationship of their father in the Gospel of Jesus. But there is a sense in which we too must become as little children, ere we can learn this sweet lesson of abiding in Him.

The little child is not self-confident: it fears the untried and unknown; it seeks the companionship of mother or friend; and it is willing to be led. Oh for the child-heart, with its simplicity and trust; its unbounded faith and lovely guilelessness! Many strong men may read these words who glory in their strength; but they must be converted, and become as little children, if they would learn the secret of abiding in Him. When we are emptied of our own strength and self-confidence, and are utterly beaten and broken, we shall be ready to obey this saintly counsel, which is the echo of the Master's own command— "Abide in Me!"

It is said of the great soldier Naaman that "his flesh came to him as the flesh of a little child." It was a splendid combination! The stalwart form of the man of war combined with the soft, sweet flesh of childhood. And these qualities should blend in each of us—strong and simple, manly and childlike; like David, the champion of Israel, whose heart was not haughty, or exercised in matters too great, but was like a child weaned from its mother. Such are counted by the Father as his babes; fed with the sincere milk of the Word; taught secrets which are hidden from the wise and prudent; and instructed in the art of abiding in Him.

It is not easy to abide in Christ all at once. It is the growth of years; the result of perpetual watching and self-discipline; the outcome of the blessed Spirit's tender influence on the inner life. It is not at first easy to get the creeper to entwine itself in some chosen direction. The string, and hammer, and knife, must be used; but in time it is satisfied to adopt the new and forced attitude. And the clinging of the soul to Christ comes as the result of prolonged habit and self-discipline beneath the culture of the Spirit of God.

The Holy Spirit will teach us to abide in Him. "The anointing which ye have received of Him abideth in you"; and *anointing* is always used as a symbol of the Spirit's grace. *"And even as it hath taught you, ye shall abide in Him."* This blessed art is taught by the Holy Spirit to those who are willing— eager—to learn. Never leave your room in the morning without lifting up your heart to Him and saying, "Teach me, O blessed Spirit, to abide in Christ for to-day: keep me in abiding fellowship with Him; even when I am not directly thinking of Him, may I be still abiding." Expect that He will do this. And when drifting from these moorings lift up your heart and say, "O my Lord, who art the Life and Light of men, give me more of thy Spirit, that I may better abide in Thee."

Abiding in Christ does not mean that you must always be thinking about Christ. You are in a house, abiding in its enclosure or beneath its shelter, though you are not always thinking about the house itself. *But you always know when you leave it.* A man may not be always thinking of his sweet home circle; but he and they may nevertheless be abiding in each other's love. And he knows instantly when any of them is in danger of passing out of the warm tropic of love into the arctic region of separation. So we may not always be sensible of the revealed presence of Jesus; we may be occupied with many things of necessary duty—but as soon as the heart is disengaged it will become aware that He has been standing near all the while; and there will be a bright flash of recognition, and a repetition of the Psalmist's cry, "Thou art near, O Lord!" Ah, life of bliss, lived under the thought of his presence; as dwellers in Alpine valleys live beneath the solemn splendour of some grand snow-capped range of mountains!

Abiding in Christ means a life of converse with Him. To tell Him all; to talk over all anxieties and occurrences with Him; to speak with Him aloud as to a familiar and interested friend; to ask his counsel or advice; to stop to praise, to adore, and utter words of love; to draw heavily upon his resources, as the branch on the sap and life of the vine; to be content to be only a channel, so long as his power and grace are ever flowing through; to be only the bed of a stream hidden from view beneath the hurrying waters, speeding without pausing towards the sea. This is abiding in Christ; this is what David must have meant when he said, "One thing have I desired of the Lord, that will I seek after, that I may dwell in the house of the Lord all the days of my life: to behold the beauty of the Lord, and to inquire in his temple."

When this abiding is secured, the root will supply all needed power in fruit-bearing. Methinks I have overheard the branches complaining that it is quite impossible to expect from them the ruddy clusters of the autumn. "Alas!" they sigh, "if you look for fruit from us, you are expecting impossibilities: we can never produce it." But they are not expected to produce it; they have only to be still, and let the root pour its tides of sap through their open ducts. And it will be discovered in blessed experience that there need be no striving, no effort, no "must" in the matter; but that spontaneously and naturally and easily the juices of the plant will break forth into manifestation, and will swell into the luscious cluster of purple grapes. The difficulty will not be in bearing, but in not bearing. There is a whole heaven of difference between *fruit* and *works* —the fruits of the Spirit, and the works of the flesh.

Oh that Christian people would learn that there is a great danger in their putting forth their own self-directed energies in Christian living; and that their true power consists in being still, while Jesus from his hidden life in heaven pours out through them his grace and power and blessing on the world.

This is the true cure for depression on the one hand, and for pride on the other. For depression: because however weak we are, our weakness cannot be a barrier to the forth-putting of his might. Indeed, it will be the chosen condition of its greatest manifestation; for surely more glory will accrue to Him, if He produces much fruit through those from whom no such results could otherwise have been anticipated. For pride: because clearly the branch cannot exalt itself as the creator of the fruit, when it has been simply the channel through which the fruit has been produced.

The whole life of the vine with its fruitful boughs is a parable of self-sacrifice. The one aim of its existence is to bear fruit, "to cheer God and man." Not even rule over the trees is to be compared with this (Judges ix. 13). And the passion which fills the heart of Jesus, and of us also, if we have drunk into his spirit, is to bear fruit for the glory of the Father, in the blessing and salvation of men. Our Lord is set on revealing to men those hidden beauties of the nature of God, with which He has been familiar from before the birth of time; and He communicates this desire to his true disciples (John xv. 8).

It is clear, therefore, that our pleasure and plans and personal gains must all be laid aside in order that this purpose may be secured. It was said by James Hinton, who had seen deeply into the heart of Christ, "If God could give us the best and greatest gift, that which above all others we might long for and aspire after, even though in despair, it is this—that He must give us the privilege He gave his Son, to be used and sacrificed for the best and greatest end." But how few of us have really entered into the spirit of this thought! We seek our life; we hedge ourselves about; we are ambitious to get a brief power; we give to others what we can easily spare. And so we lose from our lives their joy and power. But if we could but learn to efface ourselves in daily, hourly self-sacrifice, always considering what Jesus desires to do by us, and what will best promote the highest welfare of earth's weary and toiling myriads, then our joy would be full; we should live at the well-head of life; we should climb with elastic steps those higher levels of experience, where men may see the pavement of sapphire stones and the clearness of the light of heaven.

XIV

THE SECRET OF STRENGTH
(GENESIS XLIX. 24)

"My faith looks up to claim that touch divine
Which robs me of this fatal strength of mine,
And leaves me wholly resting, Lord, on thine.

"Yea, make me such an one as Thou canst bless;
Meet for thy use, through very helplessness—
Thine, only thine, the glory of success."
LUCY A. BENNETT.

As the battle swept over the fatal field of Mount Gilboa, on which David wished that no dew might ever fall again, as if to mark his horror at the tragedy enacted there, we are told that "the battle went sore against Saul, and the archers hit him; and he was sore wounded of the archers." A side-light is thus cast on the dying words of Jacob, in which he referred to the cruelty and malignity which had followed his beloved Joseph from childhood. "The archers," said the old man, "have sorely grieved him, and shot at him, and hated him." One can almost see the faces of those bitter foes, stern with cruel hate, the bow-strings drawn tight back against their ears, as they hotly follow on the steps of their prey, and sorely grieve him.

Is it not marvellous then that he should be able to add, "but his bow abode in strength"? It is one of those strange paradoxes, of which there are so many instances in Scripture. Here are some of them: "The lame take the prey"; "When I am weak, then I am strong"; "God hath chosen the weak things of the world to confound the things which are mighty." These are specimens of many more, in which the natural weakness and impotence of the mortal is nevertheless made sufficient to withstand the onsets of the foe, and hurl them back, becoming more than victorious.

Has not this been also proved true in our own experience? We too are weak enough, sorely pressed by our foes, and sometimes almost driven to despair. And yet we have continued until now; nay, we have been enabled to abide in some measure of strength. The foe has not prevailed. At the moment when he seemed on the point of victory, he has suddenly been compelled to give way; his legions have been scattered as by the invisible, but irresistible breath of God. The fire has burned under water. One has chased a thousand; and two have put ten thousand to flight.

The secret it not a hidden one. It is clearly revealed in the following words, which tell us that

> *"The arms of his hands were made strong*
> *By the hands of the mighty God of Jacob."*

It is a beautiful picture. There stands the weak child in whose slender arms there are no muscles strong enough to draw the string or bend the bow, which he vainly tries to use. They resist his utmost endeavours. Evidently he has neither might nor strength.

But now see, on his weak hands there are laid other hands, mighty hands, hands that wove the tapestry of the heavens, and that hold in their hollows the depths of the seas: one of these is placed where the left hand holds the bow; the other where the right hand plucks the string. And now with what ease those thin hands wield the bow; it is a plaything in their grasp; and without apparent strain the arrow flies to its mark. Is not this what David meant in after-days, when he sang,

> *"He teacheth my hands to war*
> *So that a bow of steel is broken*
> *By mine arms"?*

There is another Old Testament incident, which gives a vivid illustration and enforcement of these striking words. Elisha was near his end. His had been a mighty life. Like a war-chariot with its fiery steeds he had brought deliverance to his fatherland. What wonder then, in that sad time when disasters were falling thick and fast on Israel and the royal house, that the king came down for a final word of cheer and help. The answer of the dying seer was remarkable. It seemed as if the heart of a soldier had beaten under his prophet's robe, and that the ruling passion had flamed up strong in death.

"Take bow and arrows," said he. "And the king took unto him bow and arrows." Then as the king put his strong muscular sun-browned hands on the bow, the old man put his above them, and the two shot the arrow of the Lord's deliverance through the window opened toward the sun-rising, where beyond the Jordan valley the land of the Syrians lay.

Perhaps this touching incident would have better illustrated the words of Jacob, if the chill hands of the dying prophet had been under the warm powerful palms of the king. But still the main point is to notice the combination; and to see how weakness becomes able for deeds of strength, when it permits itself to be moulded, guided, wielded, used, by the hands of a mighty man of valour.

The Apostle, who was the most like Christ, and the best loved, tells us a secret when he says, "Our fellowship is with the Father, and with his Son, Jesus Christ." And the word rendered *fellowship* might be translated *partnership*; the common interests into which the saintly heart may enter with the mighty God. Ah, what a combination is here! We cannot; but He can! Our weakness supplemented by his Strength! Our impotence married in immortal union with his Omnipotence. Here, indeed, is a compensating balance. The less there is of us, and the feebler our condition, the greater scope is there for the forth-putting of a Might before which cables snap as stalks of straw; and by which opposition is swept away as the cob-web swung across the garden path is caught on the dress of the impetuous child rushing along in an ecstasy of exuberant life.

The old legend tells us that Ulysses, returning home after long years, proved his identity by bending a bow which had defied the efforts of the stoutest heroes who had tried it in his absence. There are a good many of these defiant bows lying all around us. Tasks that deride our puny efforts; empty churches that will not fill; wicked neighbourhoods that will not yield; hardened soils that will not admit the ploughshare to cut into their crust. The one thing of which we need to assure ourselves is—whether it be God's will for us to take them in hand: if not, it is useless to attempt the task; we may as well husband and reserve our strength. But if it is made clear to us that we are to take up armour, methods, instrumentalities, once wielded by giant-hands, but now as unbefitting these poorer times as the armour of the age of chivalry mocks at the smaller make of modern warriors—let us not hesitate for a single moment, let us assume the armour of defence and the weapons of attack; and, as we do so, we shall become aware of a strength being infused into us—not ours, but his: "the arms of our hands will be made strong by the hands of the mighty God of Jacob."

The condition of this strength is our consciousness of utter weakness. We are too strong for God. Our self-confidence shuts Him out of our lives. We require to be taken down to Gideon's brook, that we may be reduced to the minimum of our own energy, and be filled to the maximum of his. It was this that made Paul glory in his infirmities, where other men would have thought their infirmities debarred them from Christian usefulness. He accounted that they were the greater reason for anticipating success. Tell him that his words lacked eloquence, or that his appearance was unprepossessing, or that his thorn in the flesh made him a cripple in Christ's army— he would have answered, "I rejoice in them all—nay, I glory in them. All hail, ye blessed arguments for self-abasement, and for reckoning more completely on the mighty power of Christ!"

Do not longer assume that you cannot bend the bow of difficulty lying at your feet. You cannot do it alone; but God and you can do it together. Only do not try to feel able to do it before you take it up. You will never feel strong enough; but when you take it in hand and try to bend it, you will discover that as your day so is your strength. In the act of getting up, the paralysed man received strength to stand. Act as if you had omnipotent power; and you will discover that you have it allied with you, and working through you, to the accomplishment of purposes of which you had not dared to dream in the wildest flights of fancy.

"All power," said our Lord, "is given to Me in heaven and on earth: go ye therefore, and teach." And it is added, with blessed emphasis, by another evangelist, and in beautiful corroboration of the spirit of these words, "They went forth and preached everywhere; the Lord working with them, and confirming the Word with signs following." This was no extraordinary circumstance; it is simply the normal state of those who have yielded themselves up as channels for the mighty God to work through their lives.

A telegraph wire may as easily carry the power generated by a Niagara as by a water-wheel, to light some distant city, or drive some vast machinery. And we can be vehicles through whom Divine power can reach a dying world. Till now our own energy and might have passed through us as a slow goods train over the metals; but they will as easily sustain the rush of the express. There is no reason why, from this moment, each earnest reader of these lines may not become a medium through whom the mighty God of Jacob shall work some marvellous exhibition of power: and when it is achieved there shall be no envy or pride; because it will be obvious that He has a perfect right to use what vessel He pleases, and the glory of the issue must be given to Him whose mind planned, and whose power executed, the fair and blessed result.

XV

THE SECRET OF BLESSEDNESS
(GENESIS XLIX. 25, 26)

"He always wins who sides with God—to him no chance is lost;
God's will is sweetest to him, when it triumphs at his cost.
Ill that He blesses is our good, and unblest good our ill;
And all is right that seems most wrong, if it be His sweet will."

F. W. FABER.

UNTO what a rapture did the old man rise when describing the blessedness of his favourite son. Indeed his language failed him. His words staggered beneath the weight of meaning with which he charged them. Reverting to the blessings which his progenitors had invoked on their first-born sons, and recalling the memorable words which in that strange moment of mingled emotion the patriarch Isaac had uttered years before over his own bowed head, he declared that his blessings prevailed above the blessings of all who had preceded him. And then, as old men will, he travelled away from the flat sand plains of Egypt, unbroken by mound or hill, to the mountainous country of his earliest years, and avowed that his desire for the blessedness of Joseph reared itself above all other, as the everlasting hills tower up above the plains lying outspread at their feet.

But even though he had gone on to heap metaphor on metaphor, hyperbole on hyperbole, he could have given but vague hints of that weight of glory and blessedness which are ours in Him of whom Joseph was an imperfect representative and type. Yea, even the multiplied Beatitudes of Deut. xxviii. do but furnish the barest outlines for us to fill in with colours borrowed from the palettes of the Gospels and Epistles. The

THE SECRET OF BLESSEDNESS

last glimpse that the Apostolic band caught of the ascending Lord was with the outspread hands of blessing. So He left us: so He continues through the ages. He still sits on the Mount, calling his disciples unto Him, and saying "Blessed." And in the Apocalypse there are several additional Beatitudes recorded, part of a great multitude which no man can number, ever proceeding from his dear lips. "Blessed be the God and Father of our Lord Jesus Christ, who hath blessed us with all spiritual blessings in heavenly places in Christ."

THE BLESSINGS OF DAILY HELP.—"The God of thy father shall help thee." The earthly father must die; but the Heavenly Father abides as a very present and unfailing help. In every emergency we may hear His still small voice hushing our fear, and saying—

> *"Fear thou not; for I am with thee:*
> *I the Lord thy God will hold thy right hand,*
> *Saying unto thee,*
> *Fear not, I will help thee."*

Well then may we join with one sacred writer in boldly saying, "The Lord is my helper; and I will not fear what man shall do unto me"; and with the Apostle, who more than most had learnt to lean hard on God's helpfulness, "Having, therefore, obtained help of God, I continue unto this day."

God's help does not, for the most part, come miraculously or obviously. It steals as gradually into our life as the grass of spring clothes the hills with fresh and verdant robes. Before men can say, "Lo, here! or lo, there!" it has suddenly entered into our need and met it. A smile, a flower, a letter, a burst of music, the picture of a bit of mountain scenery, a book, the coming of a friend—such are the ways in which God comes to our help. Not helping us far in advance, but just for one moment at a time. Not giving us a store of strength to make us proud, but supplying our need as the occasion comes. Some-

times the Almighty helps us by putting his wisdom and strength
and grace into our hearts; sometimes by manipulating circumstances in our behalf; and sometimes by inclining friends or
foes to do the very thing we need. But it matters little as to
the channel—only let us rest confidently in the certainty of
receiving what we need. It may be delayed to the last moment;
but it will come. "God shall help when the morning appeareth"
(Ps. xlvi. 5, *marg.*). If the last post has come in without bringing
the expected assistance, then wait up and expect a special mes-
senger. "There is none like unto the God of Jeshurun, who
rideth upon the heaven in thy help, and in his excellency on
the sky."

When the godly man ceaseth and the faithful fail, there is
no cry that so befits our lips as the brief ejaculation with which
the Psalmist commences Psalm xii.; and this is the response
attested by old experience, and by the spirit of inspiration:
"The God of thy father shall help thee."

THE BLESSINGS OF HEAVEN ABOVE.—All that God is and
has He has deposited in our blessed Lord Jesus, as the Trustee
and Representative of his own. "It was the good pleasure of
the Father that in Him should all the fulness dwell." And thus
it is gloriously true, that "in Him dwelleth all the fulness of
the Godhead bodily; and in Him ye are made full." (Col. i. 19;
ii. 9, 10, R.V.)

This fulness of heavenly blessing is laid up for us in Jesus,
as water is stored in Eastern countries for use through the long
drought. The only difference being that in the latter case the
sun may dry up, or the dam break, or the demand be too
great for the supply. But in the case of Christ, the stores of
grace have never ceased to brim. In spite of all the demands
made on Him by ages of needy saints He is as full at this hour
as ever. The sun may shine less brilliantly; the moon grow
withered through the ages; the course of Nature waste more
quickly than the reparative processes can renew—but the stores
of Jesus are absolutely as they were when, in the first flush of

his Ascension glory, He sat down at the right hand of the throne of God. "They shall perish; but Thou continuest: and they all shall wax old as doth a garment; and as a mantle shalt Thou roll them up—as a garment—and they shall be changed: but Thou art the same, and Thy years shall not fail" (R.V.).

The difference that exists between believers lies, not in any arbitrary distinction in the Divine allotment, for God gives to each one of us all that He has and is; and to each He says, "All that I have is thine." But the difference lies in the use which each makes of his divine portion. It is as if a wealthy father were to bequeath to each of his five sons the sum of £10,000. One of them is unable to believe that so great a sum stands to his name in the bank, and so makes no use of it at all, leads a pauper's life, and dies in an almshouse. Others have faith enough to believe that there may be £1,000 to their credit, and work up to that limit, thankful for so much, but fearing to go beyond. Whilst the fifth, and youngest, believes that the father has not promised what he could not perform, and so goes on claiming more and ever more, till his whole patrimony has been absorbed; and then he discovers that a proviso in his father's will also permits him to use all the un-employed sums which had stood in his brother's names, but which they had forborne to use. "Take the talent from him, and give it unto him which hath ten talents. For unto every one that hath shall be given; and he shall have abundance." The same unsearchable riches are for each and all: but some do not use their rightful portion; others only in part; and the number is comparatively small of those who really dip deeply into the perennial all-sufficiency of Jesus.

It is the work of the Holy Spirit to convey these heavenly blessings into the soul. From his throne our Master is ever sending fleets of heavy-laden argosies to us beneath the con-voy and guidance of the Holy Spirit, who glorifies Christ in revealing what He is, and making us the happy recipients of grace on grace.

What blessedness might be ours if only we opened all the

ports of our being to the heavenly merchantmen bearing in to us from all the winds of heaven! It would be in the inner realm, as it is said to have been in Jerusalem in the days when Hiram's navy brought to it the wealth of the Orient: "And the king made silver to be in Jerusalem as stones; and cedars made he to be as the sycamore trees that are in the vale, for abundance."

We are to be in this world as our Master was: we are to have a similar access to the throne of grace, and the same power in prayer; to share his joy, his peace, his power; to be the members of the body through which He works, and on which He expends tender care in nourishing and cherishing it; to be called his friends, to whom He confides those secret things which his Father makes known to Him. We are to be so filled with all the fulness of God; so strong, and healthy, and robust, that there shall not be "one feeble person" in all the host, but that "the feeble shall be as David, and the house of David as God, as the angel of the Lord before them." All this is God's intention for us, and might be ours if only we would arise to claim by faith that which is ours by the gift of our Heavenly Father, and the purchase of the precious blood.

THE BLESSINGS OF THE UNDERLYING DEEP.—In all likelihood these words refer to some kind of thought that underneath the surface of the earth there lie vast deeps of water which supply "the brooks of water, of fountains, and depths that spring out of valleys and hills."

There is physical truth in this; and, above all, spiritual truth. For the depths have also blessings for us. The deep things of God, which pass the comprehension of the natural man: which eye hath not seen, no ear heard, nor the heart conceived; but which God hath prepared for them that wait for Him, and revealed to them that love Him—what deeps are these! The deep of his Eternal prescience and counsel. The deep of his covenant, spanning with rainbow arc the dark mystery of evil, and ordered in all things and sure. The deep of a love which would descend to shame and agony; willing rather to bear our sin than to lose us. The deep of his marvellous patience, which tires not amid our fretful petulance and frequent backslidings. Ah, what deeps are these! Deep calls unto deep, as wave challenges wave; and the Atlantic calls across the Isthmus of Panama to the mighty Pacific, the ocean of the thousand isles. Here is food for thought! How foolish are we so to feed the outer sense, that the spiritual vision becomes darkened through disuse; and we get to know so little of the great abyss which we call God, which engirdles us as a summer sea does the coral islet floating upon its breast. These are things into which angels desire to look, and stoop that they may behold; but we unfortunately refuse to imitate them, and, reversing the Apostle's attitude, look at the things which are seen, rather than at the things which are not seen, and which are eternal. "The deep that lieth under!"

THE BLESSINGS OF CHILDREN.—The Eastern glories in the number of his children. "Blessed is the man that hath his quiver full of them," is the glad response to the primal command, "Be fruitful, and multiply, and replenish the earth." Nor was there any need to dread the multiplication of children in a land where shepherds were needed for flocks, and high-born maidens did not shrink from what we should call menial work. And then there were abundant spaces on the rolling pasture-lands, or on the lone hillsides, for the vast expansion of the arts of life; and for husbandry and tillage. Under such circumstances children were indeed welcome for the defence and aggrandisement of family life; and such thoughts must have been in the heart of the dying man.

And there is a sense in which we may say that God has no higher blessing to give than to allow us to look on many spiritual children. To be greeted as the instrument of the salvation of many who but for us had never known Christ and his salvation; to anticipate the moment of standing with them before God, saying, "Behold, I and the children whom the

Lord hath given me"; to think of the ever-widening circles of influence which must spread from any one soul truly born for our Redeemer: is there under the sun a purer joy than this? But this blessing is within our reach, through the grace of God.

We must never forget, however, *the condition on which all these blessings depend.* "They shall be on the crown of the head of him that was separate from his brethren." We must not expect that we can have these choice blessings from God, unless we devote ourselves exclusively to Him and to his service. He gives his prizes, as the world gives its, to those who devote themselves wholly to their pursuit. Joseph was not only separated from his brethren and father by the distance which lay between Egypt and Canaan, but by the temper of his mind when he lived amongst them. Their aims were not his; nor his theirs. His heart was absorbed with motives and desires which found no place in theirs, or which would have been treated as unwelcome intruders. And it was this consciousness which embittered them against him, and led to his violent expulsion from their midst. The citizens of Vanity Fair cannot away with pilgrims, whose garb is outlandish, whose faces are set on a goal beyond their city, and who hasten through their streets, crying, "We buy the truth."

We, too, must come out and be separate; not adopting any particular style of dress, but cultivating the inner temple, which confesses that its true home lies beyond the stars; that its aim is to do the will of God; and that its loftiest ambition is to have the smile of the Master's glad "Well done!"

And when once the will has assumed this position, surrendering many things for the one thing—not only is there a great peace in the heart, but there is a growing appreciation of the blessings which we have so inadequately portrayed. They seem to bulk more largely on the vision; to become more real, and precious, and satisfactory; until they engross the soul with their rapturous fascination into an even greater separation from the passing shows of time. These two tempers act and re-act. On the one side we choose the blessedness of the separated life, because God bids us: and on the other, the more we know of it, the more we are weaned away from the delights with which the world attracts its votaries; and we say with the Psalmist, "Lord, my heart is not haughty, nor mine eyes lofty; neither do I exercise myself in great matters, or in things too high for me. Surely I have behaved and quieted myself, as a child that is weaned of his mother: my soul is even as a weaned child."

XVI

Joseph's Last Days and Death
(Genesis l. 24, 25)

"Twilight and evening bell,
And after that the dark;
And may there be no sadness of farewell
When I embark.

"For when from out our bourne of time and place,
The flood shall bear me far,
I hope to see my Pilot face to face,
When I have crossed the bar."
                                          TENNYSON.

"GOD will surely visit you, and ye shall carry up my bones from hence." These were the dying words of Joseph. And it is somewhat remarkable that these are the only words in his whole career which are referred to in the subsequent pages of the Scriptures. His life was a noble one, and, with one exception, the most fascinating in the sacred record; but this last dying speech is singled out from all the rest for special notice of the Holy Ghost. Of course, I refer to those words in Heb. xi., where it is said, "By faith Joseph, when he died, made mention of the exodus of the children of Israel; and gave commandment concerning his bones."

Let us notice:

I.—THE CIRCUMSTANCES UNDER WHICH THESE WORDS WERE SPOKEN. *Joseph was now an old man.* One hundred and ten years had stolen away his strength, and left deep marks upon his form. It was three and ninety years since he had been lifted from the pit to become a slave. Eighty years had passed since he had first stood before Pharaoh in all the beauty and wisdom of his young manhood. And sixty years had left their papyrus records in the State archives, since, with all the pomp and splendour of Egypt's court, he had carried the remains of his old father to Machpelah's ancient cave. So old was he that he saw the bright young faces of his great-grandchildren: "they were brought up upon Joseph's knees." With long life and many days God had blessed his faithful servant. And now, stooping beneath their weight, he was fast descending to the break-up of natural life.

But the shadows of his own decay were small compared with those which he saw gathering around his beloved people. Sixty years before, when Jacob gathered up his feet upon his bed and died, his favourite son was in the zenith of his glory. The days of mourning for the patriarch, just because he was Joseph's father, were only two less in number than those of a king. There was no difficulty in obtaining from Pharaoh the necessary permission to go three hundred miles to inter the remains beside those of Abraham and Sarah, of Isaac and Rebekah, and of Leah.

And, indeed, that funeral procession must have been of a sort not often seen. There was not only the family of Israel, but the officers of the court, and all the elders of the land of Egypt. In other words, the proud and titled magnates of Egypt, the most exclusive aristocracy in the world, were willing to follow the remains of a shepherd and a Jew to their last resting-place, out of honour for his son. "There also went up chariots and horsemen, so that it was a very great company."

But sixty years had brought great changes of which there is evidence in the text. When Jacob died all was bright; and he was honoured with a splendid funeral, because he had given to the land of Egypt so great a benefactor and saviour in the person of his son; but when Joseph died, all was getting dark, and the shadow of a great eclipse was gathering over the destinies of his people. No notice seems to have been taken in Egypt of his death. No splendid obsequies were voted to him at public expense. No pyramid was placed at the disposal of his sons. And he addresses his brethren gathered about him as being sorely in need of help. It is as if he had said: "I have done my best for you, but I am dying; nevertheless God will fill my place, and do for you all, and more than all, that I would have done myself." There is a tone of comfort in these words, which indicates how much they needed an advocate at court, and an assurance of Divine visitation.

Three hundred years before, the great founder of the nation had watched all day beside an altar, scaring away the vultures which, attracted by the flesh that lay upon it, hovered around. At length, as the sun went down, the watcher fell asleep—it is hard to watch with God—and in his sleep he dreamt. A dense and awful gloom seemed to enclose him, and to oppress his soul, and on it, as upon a curtain, passed successive glimpses of the future of his race—glimpses which a Divine voice interpreted to his ear. He saw them exiled to a foreign country, enslaved by the foreigner, and lingering there whilst three generations of men bloomed as spring flowers, and were cut down before the keen sickle of death. And as he beheld all the terror of that enslavement, the horror of a great darkness fell upon his soul. We know how exactly that horror was justified by the events which were so soon to take place. "The Egyptians made the children of Israel to serve with rigour: and they made their lives bitter with hard bondage, in mortar, and in brick, and in all manner of service in the field; all their service, wherein they made them serve, was with rigour." The first symptoms of that outburst of popular "Jew-hate" were already, like stormy petrels, settling about the closing hour of the great Egyptian premier.

We cannot tell the precise form of those symptoms. Perhaps he had been banished from the councils of Pharaoh; perhaps he was already pining in neglect; perhaps the murmurs of dislike against his people were already rising, just as the roar

JOSEPH'S LAST DAYS AND DEATH   153

of the breakers against a harbour-bar tells how the mighty
ocean is arousing itself to frenzy; perhaps acts of oppression
and cruelty were increasingly rife, and increasingly difficult to
bring to justice. In any case, the twilight of the dark night was
gathering in; and it was this which made his words more
splendid: they shone out as stars of hope.

Moreover, his brethren were around him. His forgiveness
and love to them lasted till the testing-hour by that great
assayer, Death. Nor did *they* fail. From something narrated in
the previous verses of this chapter, it would appear that, for
long, his brethren, judging of him by their own dark and im-
placable hearts, could not believe in the sincerity and genuineness of his forgiveness. They thought that he must be feigning
more than he felt, in order to secure some ulterior object, such
as the blessing and approval of their old father. And so they
feared that, as soon as Jacob was removed, Joseph's just
resentment, long concealed with masterly art, would break
forth against them. It seemed impossible to believe that he felt
no grudge, and would take no action at all with reference to
the past; and they said, "Joseph will certainly requite us all
the evil which we did unto him." And Joseph wept when they
spake; wept that they should have so misunderstood him after
his repeated assurances; wept to see them kneeling at his feet
for a forgiveness which he had freely given them years before.
"Fear not," said he in effect; "do not kneel there; I am not
God: ye thought evil against me; but God meant it for good,
to save much people alive, as it is this day."

This forgiveness might well be wonderful to these men; because it *was not of this world at all.* The Lord Jesus, who
lighteth every man coming into the world, was in Joseph's
heart, though less clearly in Joseph's creed; and his behaviour
was a foreshadowing of Incarnate Love. Reader! He waits to
forgive thee thus. Though thou hast maligned, and refused,
and crucified Him afresh, and put Him to an open shame; yet,
for all that, He waits to forgive thee so entirely, that not one of
these things shall be ever mentioned against thee again; yea,

if they are looked for, they shall never be found, any more than a stone can be found which has been cast into the bosom of the Atlantic waves. Oh, give Christ credit for his free and entire forgiveness! And remember that when once He forgives, it is unnecessary and distrustful to go to Him again about the same sin. He cannot forgive the same sin twice; and when once He has pronounced the Words of Absolution over a kneeling penitent, that penitent need never go to Him, as did the brethren of Joseph, and say, Forgive, I pray thee, my trespass and my sin, concerning which, Thou knowest, I came to thee with tears and sighs so many years ago.

It is said of the love of the Lord Jesus that, having loved his own, which were in the world, He loved them unto the end; or, as the margin of the Revised Version puts it, "to the uttermost." He is able to save to the uttermost, because He loves to the uttermost. So was it with the love of Joseph; it had outlived the frosts of the early spring, and it bore fruit and looked fresh now in the late autumn of his last days. Oh that we might love and forgive like this! It is possible on one condition only—viz., that we open our hearts for the entrance and indwelling of Him who, so long before his incarnation, had already found a home beneath the doublet of this great Egyptian statesman.

Lastly, he was dying. He had warded off death from Egypt; but he could not ward it off from himself. "I die." They were among the last words that he had caught from his father's dying lips (chap. xlviii. 21), and now he appropriates them to himself; yes, and in doing so, he touches the zenith of his noble confidence and hope. Oh that each of us may go on shining more and more each day until our last, and that, when heart and flesh are failing most conspicuously, the life of the spirit may flash out with its most brilliant coruscations, like the lights from Gideon's broken pitchers. There is no better proof of immortality than this: that in us must be a something more than flesh and blood, which, when these are most impaired, is most bright and most alive to the realities of the eternal world. And there must be a sphere appropriate to the ethereal tenant, who stands so keen and eager, reaching forth, with unimpaired vitality and with unquenchable vigour.

It was under all these circumstances that Joseph said, "God will surely visit you; and ye shall carry up my bones from hence."

II. LET US INVESTIGATE THE FULL IMPORTANCE OF THESE WORDS. And we may do so best by comparing them with Jacob's dying wish: "Bury me with my fathers in the cave that is in the field of Machpelah." This was most natural: we all love to be buried by the beloved dust of our departed. And Jacob knew that there would be no great difficulty in carrying out his wish. Joseph was then in the plenitude of his power. There was no great faith therefore in asking for that which could so easily be accomplished. But with Joseph it was different. He too wanted to be buried in the land of Canaan; but not at once—not then! There were two things he expected would happen: the one, that the people would go out of Egypt; the other, that they would come into the land of Canaan. He did not know when or how; he was only sure that so it would be: "surely."

To Joseph's natural vision these things were most unlikely. When he spoke, Israel was settled in Goshen, and so increasing in numbers and in wealth that any uprooting was becoming daily more unlikely. And as to the oppression which was perhaps beginning to threaten them, what chance would they have of ever being able to escape from the detaining squadrons of Egypt's chivalry, supposing they wished to go? But his anticipation of the future was not founded on human foresight, but on the distinct announcements of the Almighty. He remembered how God had said to Abraham, as he stood upon his mountain oratory, "Look from the place where thou art, northward, and southward, and eastward, and westward; for all the land that thou seest, to thee will I give it, and to they seed for ever." That promise was repeated to Isaac. "Unto thee, and

unto thy seed, will I give all these countries; and I will perform
the oath which I sware unto Abraham thy father."

Again was that promise reiterated to Jacob as he lay at the
foot of the shining ladder, "The land whereon thou liest, to
thee will I give it, and to thy seed." These promises had been
carefully treasured and handed on, as in the old Greek race
they handed on the burning torch. Jacob on his death-bed
reassured Joseph that God would certainly bring them to the
land of their fathers; and now Joseph re-animated the trembling company that gathered around him with the self-same
hope. In the memories of all these men the word spoken two
hundred years before rang like a peal of silver bells in a moss-
grown tower. "They shall come hither again" (Gen. xv. 16).
Joseph could not trace the method of the Divine workman-
ship: it was enough for him to know that God had said, "They
shall come hither again." And so he commanded that his bones
should be unburied, so that at any moment, however hurried,
when the trumpet of exodus sounded, they might be ready to
be caught up and borne onward in the glad march for Canaan.

What a lesson must those unburied bones have read to Israel!
When the taskmasters dealt hardly with the people, so that
their hearts fainted, it must have been sweet to go and look
at the mummy case which held those mouldering remains,
waiting there to be carried forward; and, as they did so, this
was doubtless their reflection, "Evidently then, Joseph believed
that we were not to stay here always, but that we should sooner
or later leave for Canaan: let us brace ourselves up to bear
a little longer, it may only be a very little while!" Yes, and
when some were tempted to settle down content with prosper-
ing circumstances, and to feast upon leeks, garlics, and onions,
it was a check on them to think of those bones, and say,
"Evidently we are not to remain here always: we should do
well not to build all our hopes and comfort on the unstable
tenure of our sojourn in this place." And, oftentimes, when the
people were ready to despair amid the difficulties and weari-
ness of their desert march, those bones borne in their midst

told them of the confident hope of Joseph—that God would bring them to the land of rest.

We have no unburied bones to animate our faith, or to revive our drooping zeal; but we have something better—we have an empty grave. Oh, what volumes does that mutely tell us! When John the Baptist died, his disciples dispersed; when Jesus died, his disciples not only clung together, but sprang up into an altogether new vigour. And well they might! And the difference was made by that empty grave in the garden of Joseph of Arimathea. And what it did for them it will do for us. It tells us that He is risen. It tells us that not death, but life, is to be the guardian angel of our desert march. It tells us that this world is not our resting place or home; but that we must seek these above, where Christ sitteth at the right hand of God. It tells us that resurrection is not possible only, but certain; and that ere long we shall be where He is. He will go with us along the desert pathway, till we go to be with Him, where the shadow of death is never flung over flower, or child, or friend.

III. Let us Realize the Spirit that Underlay and Prompted these Words. It was above all a pilgrim spirit. Joseph bore an Egyptian title. He married an Egyptian wife. He shared in Egyptian court-life, politics, and trade. But he was as much a pilgrim as was Abraham pitching his tent outside the walls of Hebron, or Isaac in the grassy plains of the south country, or Jacob keeping himself aloof from the families of the land. "He filled his place at Pharaoh's court; but his dying words open a window into his soul, and betray how little he had felt that he belonged to the order of things in the midst of which he had been content to live. Though surrounded by an ancient civilization; and dwelling among granite temples and solid pyramids and firm-based sphinxes, the very emblems of eternity; he confessed that he had here no continuing city, but sought one to come."[1]

[1] Maclaren's Sermons; second series, p. 139.

We sometimes speak as if the pilgrim-spirit were impossible for us who live in this settled state of civilization. Our houses are too substantial; our lives too unromantic; our movements too closely tethered to one narrow round. But if that thought should ever cross our hearts again, let us turn to the life of Joseph, and remind ourselves how evidently he was animated by the spirit of those "who confessed that they were pilgrims and strangers on the earth." Ah, friends, what are we living for? Are our pursuits bounded by the narrow horizon of earth, and limited to the fleeting moments of time? Are we constantly engaged in lining as warmly as possible the nest in which we hope to spend our old age and die? Are we perpetually seeking to make the best of this world? I fear me, that these are the real aims of many professing Christians; and, if so, it is simply useless for them to claim kinship with that mighty stream of pilgrims, which is constantly pouring through the earth, bound to the city which hath foundations, their true home and mother-city. On the other hand, it is quite conceivable that you may be at the head of a large establishment, engaged in many permanent undertakings, closely attached to the present by imperious duties; and yet, like Joseph, your heart may be detached from things seen and temporal, and engaged, in all its secret longings, to the things unseen and eternal.

The pilgrim-spirit will not make us unpractical. Joseph was the most practical man in his time. Who are likely to be as prompt, as energetic, as thorough, as those who feel that they are working for eternity, and that they are building up day by day a fabric in which they shall live hereafter? Each day is character-building for better or for worse: each deed, well or ill done, is a stone in the edifice; each moment tells on eternity. We shall receive a reward according to our deeds.

But the pilgrim-spirit will make us simple. There are two sorts of simplicity: that of circumstances; and that of heart. Many a man sits down to bread and milk at a wooden table, with a heart as proud as pride can make it: whilst many another who eats off a golden plate is as simple as Cincinnatus at his plough. The world cannot understand this. But here in Joseph is an illustration. Ah, my friend, it is not the unjewelled finger, nor the plain attire, nor the unfurnished room, that constitutes a simple unaffected life: but that vision of the spirit, which looks through the unsubstantial wreath-vapours of the morning to the peaks of the everlasting hills beyond and above.

What a contrast there is between the opening and closing words of Genesis! Listen to the opening words: "In the beginning, God." Listen to the closing words, "A coffin in Egypt." And is this all? Is all God's work to end in one poor mummy case? Stay. This is only the end of Genesis, the Book of Beginnings. Turn the leaf, and there are Exodus, and Joshua, and Kings, and Prophets, and Christ. God is not dependent on any one of us. We do our little work and cease, as the coral-insects which perish by myriads on the rising reef. But God's work goes on. His temple rises age after age. And it is enough for each of us, like Joseph, to have lived a true, pure, strong, and noble life—and to leave Him to see after our bodies; our beloved, whom we leave so reluctantly; and our work. Nor will He fail. "And Moses took the bones of Joseph with him," on the night of the exodus (Exod. xiii. 19); "and they buried the bones of Joseph in Shechem: . . . and it became the inheritance of the children of Joseph" (Josh. xxiv. 32).